Clair
MW01520395

Pre-Intermediate

Matters

Addison Wesley Longman Limited,
Edinburgh Gate, Harlow,
Essex CM20 2JE, England
and Associated Companies throughout the world.

© Addison Wesley Longman Limited 1996
All rights reserved; no part of this publication
may be reproduced, stored in a retrieval system,
or transmitted in any form or by any means, electronic,
mechanical, photocopying, recording or otherwise,
without the prior written permission of the Publishers.

First published in one edition 1995

First published Part B 1996

Set in Linotronic 300 ITC Garamond Light 10/12pt
and Frutiger Light 8½/10pt
by SX Composing Ltd, Rayleigh, Essex

Printed in Singapore

ISBN 0582 29784 2

Under no circumstances may any part of this book be
photocopied for resale.

Authors' Acknowledgements

We would like to thank the following people.
- Our close advisors for their constructive support:
  Marc Beeby, Gillie Cunningham, Olivia Date, Sara
  Humphreys.
- Those people who reported on and/or piloted the
  material, in particular: Jacqueline Donohoe, Rebecca
  Fong, Teresa Pego, Jacqui Robinson, Sarah Stratford,
  Liz Waters.
- Our publisher, Kate Goldrick; our Senior
  Development Editor, Sue Ullstein; our editor, Carol
  Hadwen; our designers, Marnie Searchwell, Amanda
  Easter and Jennifer Coles; as well as
  Pat Dutch (permissions editor), Susan Greer
  (secretary), Alma Gray (audio producer),
  Lisa Bondesio and Cathy May (project managers),
  Donna Wright (production controller), Diane May
  (art editor) – all at Longman ELT.
- The staffs of Bell School, Old House, in particular,
  Maria Heron, and Bell School, Saffron Walden for
  their support and advice.

Pre-Intermediate

Matters

Part B
Note that the page numbering remains the same as in the full edition of the Students' Book.

JAN BELL
ROGER GOWER

Contents chart

Grammar	Vocabulary	Dictation and Pronunciation (See Workbook)
Comparative and superlative adjectives *as ... as*	Hobbies	Spelling and the alphabet
Second Conditional	Crime	Grammar and pronunciation Sound and spelling: /v/ and /w/
Defining relative clauses: *who, which, that, where* Adjective word order *We use a ... for ...-ing*	Describing people Relationships	Rhyming words Vocabulary
Used to Question tags	Entertainment	Sound and spelling: *a*
Quantity words: *some-, any-, no-, every-* *too* and *very* *too much* and *too many*	Education	Vocabulary and word stress
The passive (Present and Past Simple)	News stories	The passive
The unfinished past: Present Perfect Continuous and Present Perfect Simple *For* and *since*	Having a party	Contrastive stress
Sentence patterns (1): verb + person + *to* + base form of the verb Sentence patterns (2): reported sentences *say* and *tell*	Doing things in the house *Do* or *make*?	Sentence completion Sound and spelling: *u*
Verb patterns (1): *if, when, as soon as, unless* Verb patterns (2): verb and 2 objects (*Give it to him. Give him the present.*)	Sports	Rhythm and sentence stress
REVISION Mixed practice Second Conditional Making comparisons Question tags	REVISION Phrasal verbs Mixed words	Sound and spelling: *g*

Word list PAGE 130   Tapescripts PAGE 132

INTRODUCTION *To the teacher*

These are some notes to help you before you begin. The Students' Book contains twenty units, each divided into six sections: Use your English, Skills, Grammar, Vocabulary, Use and review and Language reference. This is how each unit is organised.

Use your English

This section revises and extends everyday English, including useful phrases and vocabulary. The aim is to develop students' confidence in being able to communicate.

Skills

In this section students will meet natural written and spoken English and develop techniques, such as deducing new words from context, using dictionaries and so on. Vocabulary areas are extended out of the text and practised.

Controlled Writing exercises help with organisational skills (the use of linking expressions, paragraph construction etc.). Specific linguistic areas which are necessary in writing (articles, adverbs etc.) are also presented and practised.

Grammar

There is oral and written controlled practice in each unit and at the end of the unit there is the Language reference section for study. The *Using your grammar* section in each unit gives communicative oppportunities to practise the grammar presented in a less controlled way.

Vocabulary

The Vocabulary section is mainly linked to the topic of the unit and includes a *Using your vocabulary* section to activate it.

Use and review

In this section there are communicative activities which revise the grammar and vocabulary presented in the preceding units. The exception to this pattern is Unit 20 which revises the book.

Language reference

The Language reference section provides a concise summary of the language covered in each unit.

Flexibility

Pre-Intermediate Matters Students' Book can be adapted to suit different teaching programmes. It can be extended by drawing on the extra practice in the Workbook, and activities and ideas in the Teacher's Book. For short courses, certain sections can be omitted. The sections within each unit of the Students' Book have been clearly signposted throughout to enable you to do this.

We hope you will enjoy the course and look forward to hearing how you get on.

Jan Bell and Roger Gower

•Enjoying life•

USE YOUR ENGLISH

Filling in a form

1   When do you have to fill in a form?

2   When would you fill in these forms?

See the World Holidays

| HOLIDAY   BOOKING   FORM | | WINTER |

NAME

DEPARTURE AIRPORT

Application for Employment

Education

Previous experience

IMMIGRATION FORM

Please complete in BLOCK CAPITALS

Surname

First names

Address in the UK

Date of birth

Nationality

Present occupation

Length of stay

Purpose of visit

Passport number

Signature

For official use only

RENTACAR

Booking form

Driving licence number

Additional driver/s

3   Work with a partner.

a) These are the answers to questions about some of the
headings on the immigration form. What are the headings?

b) Make questions for the answers. Example:
How long are you staying in this country?

c) [🖵 11.1]   Listen. Sally Jones has just arrived at Heathrow
Airport in London. She's going through Immigration. Compare
the Immigration Officer's questions with your questions.

4   Work with a partner. He/She has come to England to study
English for three months. Ask your partner questions and fill in
the form in Exercise 2 for him/her.

1   2 weeks.

2   4 July, 1972.

3   Canadian.

4   On business.

5   Sales manager.

SKILLS

Listening and speaking

1   Philip does a lot of deep-sea diving. Look at the picture. What do you think happened to him?

rock climbing

camping

flying a plane

parachuting

2 [🖭 11.2]   Listen to Philip.

a) Were your guesses correct? Philip had a lucky escape. How?

b) Look at the pictures on the left. Which one does Philip **not** talk about?

c) Listen again. Complete the sentences with one or more words.

Philip and Sarah's lives are very _____. Once, in the Gulf of Mexico, they were _____ the bottom of the sea when Sarah _____ a shark. When she _____ her arms at Phil he thought she _____ breathe. When Phil realised what the problem was he moved _____ but the shark _____ interested and swam _____ him.

3   Find the /ʃ/ sound on the phonemic chart on page 132.

a) Which letters make the /ʃ/ sound in the word *parachuting*?

b) [🖭 11.3]   Listen to these words. Which letters make the /ʃ/ sound: information, especially, profession, finish, machine?

c) Practise saying the words. Stress the correct syllable.

4   Philip says: '*We don't spend our free time **doing crosswords**.*' Match the verbs from A with the nouns from B.

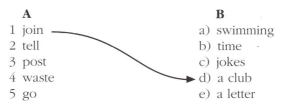

A	B
1 join	a) swimming
2 tell	b) time
3 post	c) jokes
4 waste	d) a club
5 go	e) a letter

Writing: spelling

[🖭 11.4]   Listen to ten sentences. Write the word you hear at the end of each sentence.

GRAMMAR

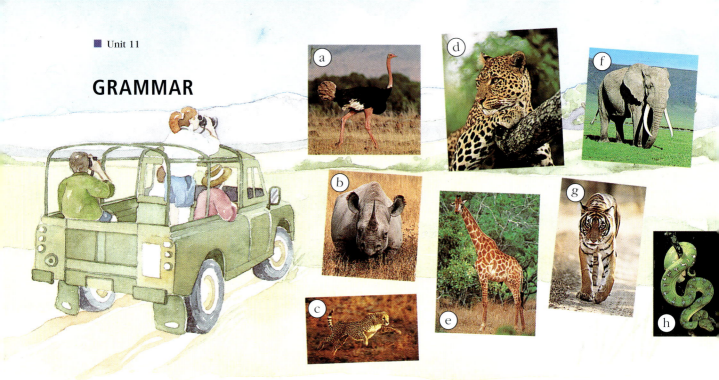

Comparatives and superlatives

1   The dream of many animal lovers is to go on safari. Look at the pictures above and answer the questions. Answers on page 126.

1 Which is faster, a leopard or a cheetah?
2 Which is more short-sighted, a rhino or a tiger?
3 Which has better hearing, a snake or a giraffe?
4 Which is heavier, an elephant or a giraffe?
5 Which animal has a longer neck, a giraffe or an ostrich?

2   Which words are the adjectives in these sentences?

1 A rhino is more short-sighted than a tiger.
2 A cheetah is faster than a leopard.
3 An elephant is heavier than a giraffe.

Comparative adjectives

When we compare two things we use the comparative form of adjectives.

a) Adjectives of one syllable: adjective + -er.
   Example: *nice → nic**er** (than)*
b) Adjectives of two syllables ending in -y:
   adjective + -ier. Example: *pretty → prett**ier** (than)*
c) Adjectives with two, three or more syllables:
   more + adjective. Example: *interesting →*
   ***more** interesting (than)*

3   Match the grammar rules a)–c) with 1–3 in Exercise 2.

4   Compare the animals in the picture. Use adjectives from the box and any other adjectives you know. Example:
A cheetah is smaller than a tiger.

small	attractive	slow	noisy	ugly
nice	beautiful	strong	dangerous	

Superlative adjectives

When we compare three or more things we use the superlative form of adjectives.

a) Adjectives of one syllable: adjective + -est.
   Example: *slow → (the) slow**est***
b) Adjectives of two syllables ending in -y:
   adjective + -iest. Example: *noisy → (the) nois**iest***
c) Adjectives with two, three or more syllables: *most* + adjective. Example: *beautiful → (the) **most** beautiful*

5   In your opinion which of the animals is:

1 the nicest?   3 the most dangerous?
2 the ugliest?   4 the best swimmer?

6   What are the comparative and superlative forms of these adjectives?

	Comparative	Superlative
1 good	_____	the _____
2 bad	_____	the _____
3 hot	_____	the _____

Check your guesses in the *Language reference* on page 71.

Making comparisons

When we make comparisons we can also use:
a) *as* + adjective + *as*. Example:
  She's **as** old **as** I am (we are the same age).
b) *Not as* + adjective + *as*. Example:
  She is**n't as** old **as** I am (we are not the same age).

7 Use *as ... as* and *not as ... as* to make comparisons.
Example: towns / cities *(big)*
Towns aren't as big as cities.

1 milk / ice-cream *(fattening)*
2 reading a novel / watching a film on TV *(enjoyable)*
3 spiders / snakes *(horrible)*
4 men / women *(emotional)*

8 [🔊 11.5] Listen and disagree with these sentences. Example:
A: Spring's wetter than autumn.
B: *No, spring isn't as wet as autumn.*

9 Complete these sentences. Use the comparative or superlative form of the adjective in brackets or *(not) as ... as.*

1 Hang-gliding is *more exciting than* reading a book. *(exciting)*
2 I weigh over 100 kilos. You're _____ me! *(light)*
3 I think jazz is _____ rock music. *(good)*
4 The necklace wasn't _____ I thought. *(expensive)*
5 You look _____ you did yesterday. *(bad)*
6 What's _____ month of the year? *(wet)*
7 My _____ holiday was in Cuba. *(enjoyable)*
8 Is cheese _____ meat? *(healthy)*
9 Schooldays are _____ days of your life! *(good)*

Using your grammar

1 Compare the following. Use comparative and superlative forms. Examples: walking, jogging, running
Running is harder than jogging.
Walking is more relaxing than running.
Jogging every morning is the best thing for your health.

1 living in a flat, living in an hotel, living in a house
2 playing cards, skiing, sleeping
3 learning a foreign language, learning to ride a horse, learning to cook
4 going shopping, visiting museums, going to a disco
5 travelling by train, travelling by plane, travelling by car

2 Compare these people. Use the words in the box. Example:
Anne is tidier than Bill.

Bill

Anne

Susan and Alan

Jeff and Joan

friendly	funny	hard-working	quiet	polite
good-looking	young	tidy	sociable	old-fashioned

3 Work in groups. Compare the people in your class.

a) Give yourself a mark from 1 to 5 for the following:
  tall (1 = not tall; 5 = very tall), fit, old, tidy, hard-working.
b) Who is:

1 the tallest?   3 the oldest?   5 the most untidy?
2 the fittest?   4 the tidiest?   6 the most hard-working?

VOCABULARY

Hobbies

1   Work with a partner. Here are some things you can do in your free time. Match words from A and B.

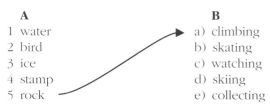

A	B
1 water	a) climbing
2 bird	b) skating
3 ice	c) watching
4 stamp	d) skiing
5 rock	e) collecting

2   Look at the pictures on the right.

a) Think of a hobby for each picture.
b) What other hobbies do you know?
c) Which hobby is the most:

- enjoyable? • exciting? • expensive? • dangerous?
- unusual? • relaxing? • energetic? • popular?

3   What do we call the people who do these things?

HOBBY	PERSON
dancing	'dancer
cycling	_____
photography	_____
cooking	_____
music	_____
acting	_____

Mark the stressed syllable in each word.

Using your vocabulary

1   What do you like doing in your free time? Use expressions like: *I'm quite keen on / I like / I enjoy walking.*

2   Prepare a short talk about hobbies. Choose a hobby from Exercises 1–3 above which you would like to try. Then choose a hobby you would not like to try. Give your reasons. Make notes.

3   Work in groups. Give your talk to the group.

USE AND REVIEW

1   Antonio has just arrived in Britain. What should he say in these situations? Use the words in brackets. Example: he wants to buy a pair of trousers. (try on / pay by cheque?)
Could I try these trousers on ? Can I pay by cheque?

He wants to:

1 book a table at a restaurant. *(reserve a table by the window / 4 people / 6 o'clock?)*
2 order food at a restaurant. *(chicken and salad / red wine?)*
3 pay the bill at a restaurant. *(bill / take Visa / service included?)*
4 start a conversation with a young woman at a disco. *(here / often?)*
5 invite a friend to the cinema. *(fancy?)*
6 invite someone he doesn't know very well to the cinema. *(like?)*

2   Where would Antonio hear these expressions? Match the expressions in A with the places in B.

A	B
1 Day return, please.	a) in a baker's
2 Three second class stamps, please.	b) at a railway station
3 How would you like your money?	c) in a post office
4 I'd like a small white loaf, please	d) in a bank

3   What other things can you tell Antonio about Britain? Example: *when the British say 'Cheers'* or *when the British shake hands.*

4   Work with a partner. Antonio wants to visit *your* country. What should he say and do there?

Language reference

1 Comparatives

FORM

For adjectives which end with one vowel followed by one consonant, double the consonant in the comparative form.
   *hot →   hot**ter** (than)*
Note the irregular forms.
   *good → **better** (than)*
   *bad → **worse** (than)*

USE

We use comparatives when we compare two things.
   *A train is fast**er** than a bus.*

2 Superlatives

FORM

a) For adjectives of one syllable, add *-est* at the end in the superlative form.
   *young→ the young**est***

b) For adjectives which end in one vowel + one consonant, double the consonant and add *-est* at the end.
   *hot → the hot**test***
   Note the irregular forms:
   *good → the **best***
   *bad → the **worst***

USE

We use superlatives when we compare three or more things.
   *April is the wet**test** month of the year.*

3 *as* + adjective + *as*

When we make comparisons we can also use *as* + adjective + *as* (which means the same or equal) or *not as* + adjective + *as* (which means not the same or not equal).
   *My hands are **as** cold **as** ice. (My hands are cold. Ice is cold. My hands are like ice.)*
   *He's not **as** strong **as** I am. (We are not equal. I am stronger. He is weaker.)*

•Witness•

USE YOUR ENGLISH

Making conversation

1   These people are at a party.

a) [📼 12.1]   Listen and match the conversations with the couples.

b) Listen again and complete these sentences from each conversation.
  1 I'm _____ now, _____ . How _____ ?
  2 You're _____.
  3 I _____ think _____. I haven't seen him.
  4 I _____. We're playing football later.

c) In some of the conversations the people are pleased to see each other. In which conversations? How do you know?

2   Answer these questions about Conversation 4.
1 Is it going to snow? What does the woman think?
2 Does the man want snow? Why/ Why not?

3   What would you say in these situations?
Which is the correct answer?
1 A: Do you think it'll be hot tomorrow?
  B: *I hope so. / I hope not.* We're on holiday.
2 A: Have we got any milk in the fridge?
  B: *I think so. / I don't think so.* I bought three bottles yesterday.

4   Work with a partner.

a) Complete each conversation with one of these expressions.

> I hope so.

> I don't think so.

> I think so.

> I hope not.

1 A: Let's go for a picnic.
  B: Do you think it's going to stay sunny?
  A: Yes, _____. The weather looks very good.
2 A: Hurry up!
  B: Have we missed the train?
  A: _____. It's the last one today.
3 A: It's freezing in this room.
  B: Is there a heater?
  A: _____. I can't find one.
4 A: I passed all my exams.
  B: Well done! Are you going to university?
  A: _____. I want to go very much.

b) Practise each conversation.

Missing

YESTERDAY PAT WENT BACK to her normal job as a policewoman. But for a year she was close, very close, to a man who told her he had killed his wife. Keith Brown didn't know Pat was a policewoman. And he fell in love with her.

So what happened? In the summer of 1992 Brown and his wife had a furious argument. The neighbours heard everything. After that day no one saw his wife again. The police were sure Keith Brown had killed her but he refused to answer any questions.

Early in October, Brown answered a lonely-hearts advertisement in the Sun Valley Times. The woman who put the advertisement in the newspaper telephoned the police. She told them about Keith Brown's letter to her. The police decided that policewoman Pat, not the woman, should meet Keith Brown. Pat phoned Keith Brown – the first of many telephone conversations about life and love, and about his wife.

They had their first meeting in a pub in Preston. The police could listen to Brown's conversation with Pat because she had a small microphone inside her dress. Brown and Pat met five more times and he fell in love with her. On February 25, 1993, Brown asked her to live with him. She said: "I can't live with you. Your wife might come home at any time." Pat wanted to end their relationship.

But she agreed to meet Brown once more. While they were talking, Brown suddenly confessed. He told Pat, "My wife will never come home again. I killed her. Voices in my head told me to kill her. I'm sorry. I love you. I want to spend my life with you." Again, the police recorded everything. They arrested Brown.

But the judge did not accept Brown's confession as evidence. Although Brown confessed that he had killed his wife, he went free.

And Pat? She has moved to another job.

SKILLS

Reading and speaking

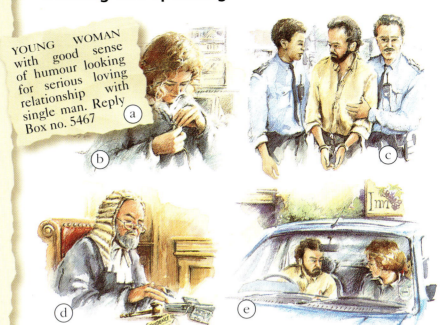

YOUNG WOMAN with good sense of humour looking for serious loving relationship with single man. Reply Box no. 5467

1   Look at the pictures above. They tell the story of Keith Brown and a woman called Pat. Match the sentences with the pictures.
1 The *lonely-hearts advertisement* which Keith Brown read.
2 The police are *arresting* Keith Brown.
3 Keith Brown is *confessing* that he *killed* his wife.
4 Pat is going to *record* Keith Brown's words on her *microphone*.
5 The *judge* is listening to the *evidence*.

2   What do you think happened?

3   Read the article on the left and check your answers.

4   Read the article again. Are these sentences *True* (T) or *False* (F)?
1 The police found the body of Brown's wife in the summer.
2 Brown said his wife left him.
3 Pat put a lonely-hearts advertisement in the newspaper.
4 Pat and Brown first met in a pub.
5 Pat had a secret microphone.
6 Pat said to Brown, 'Keith, I want to live with you.'
7 The judge sent Brown to prison.

5   Do you agree with these sentences? Why/ Why not?
1 The judge was wrong not to accept the evidence.
2 What the police did to catch Keith Brown was a good idea.
3 I could do what Pat did.

Vocabulary

Look at these nouns from the article on page 73: *conver'sation, 'meeting, ad'vertisement.*
Make the verbs in the box into nouns with one of these endings: *-ation, -ing, -ment.* Example: *improvement.*

improve	feel	argue
examine	save	explain
pronounce	warn	

Writing: *the*

> The woman put an advertisement in **the** Sun Valley Times.
>
> We use **the** when we know there is only one:
> **the** Times   **the** sun
> **the** President   **the** Pacific
> **the** Eiffel Tower   **the** River Nile
> **the** National Gallery
> **the** United Nations
>
> We do not use **the** before:
> • continents (Africa)
> • most countries (France, Brazil, Indonesia, but the USA, the UK)
> • languages (Spanish)
> • mountains (Mount Everest, Mont Blanc but the Alps, the Himalayas)
> • towns (Preston)
> • street names (Oxford Street)
> • stations and airports (Heathrow)
> • meals (I've had breakfast)

Cross out *the* in these conversations where necessary.
1 A: Have you been to ~~the~~ Italy?
   B: Yes. It's the only country in the Europe I would like to live in. I also speak the Italian.
2 A: What's the name of the place you're moving to?
   B: The Oldham.
   A: Oh, I was born there.
   B: We've bought a house in the Park Road near the river.

GRAMMAR

The Second Conditional

Jane is filling in a questionnaire in a magazine. Read the first part of the questionnaire and her answers.

ARE YOU HONEST?

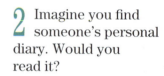

1 Imagine you find £20 sticking out of a cash machine. Would you give it to the bank?

If I found £20 sticking out of a cash machine, I would keep it. I wouldn't give it to the bank.

2 Imagine you find someone's personal diary. Would you read it?

Yes, if I found someone's personal diary, I'd read it.

1   Look at Jane's answer to question 1 again.
1 Has Jane found £20 or is she imagining it?
2 Is she talking about the past, the present or the future?
3 What verb form is *found*?
4 Compare Jane's answer with this sentence:
   If I find £20, I'll keep it.
   In which sentence does Jane think it is possible that she will find £20?

2   Read Jane's answers to questions 1 and 2 again and complete this rule.
In the Second Conditional, the *if* part of the sentence often has the _____ form of the verb. In the other part of the sentence, the base form of the verb follows _____.

3 Jane didn't finish her answers to questions 3 and 4 of the questionnaire.
Complete her answers with the correct form of the verb. Use *would, wouldn't* or *'d* where necessary.

3 Imagine a friend asks your opinion about the clothes he/she is wearing. You think he/she looks terrible. Would you tell him/her?

No, if a friend (ask) _____ me my opinion about the clothes he was wearing, I (not, say) _____ he looked terrible. I (lie) _____.

4 Imagine you book into an expensive hotel. There is a wonderful towel in your bathroom. Would you steal it?

If I (book) _____ into an expensive hotel and there (be) _____ a wonderful towel in the bathroom, I (not, steal) _____ it. I (leave) _____ it.

4 Work with a partner. Are you honest? Ask and answer the questions in the questionnaire.

**carry on here
03.03.99**

Using your grammar

1 Work with a partner. How would you spend your perfect weekend? Ask each other questions. Example: Where / go?
Where would you go?
1 Who / go with?
2 How / get there?
3 Where / stay?
4 What / have to eat and drink?
5 What / like to do?
6 Who / send a postcard to?

2 Work with a partner. What would you do, think or feel in these situations? Example: Your house is on fire.
If my house was on fire, I'd phone the fire station. I'd be very upset.
1 You are a famous person.
2 You meet the US President in the street.
3 You win a million dollars in a competition.
4 You can have any job you like.
5 You have to change your name.
6 You can live where you like.

3 If you had your life again, would you prefer to be a man or a woman? Tell your partner and give your reasons.

4 Work in two groups.
GROUP A
Write the questions for a quiz. Use the Second Conditional.
1 What kind of music / you sing / you be Pavarotti?
2 Which city / you go to / you want to visit the Vatican?
3 What languages / you speak / you live in Singapore?
4 Where / you be / you be at Harvard?
GROUP B
Write questions for a quiz. Use the Second Conditional.
1 Which sport / you play / you be at Wimbledon?
2 What you see / you visit the Louvre?
3 Where you be / you be at Copacabana?
4 What you do / you have a balalaika?
Now Group A asks Group B questions and Group B asks Group A questions. The group with the most correct answers wins. (See page 126.)

VOCABULARY

Crime

1 [📼 12.2]   Listen.
a) Match the stories with the pictures.

b) Which word goes with which picture?
   burglar   robber   thief

2   Complete the table. Use a dictionary to help you. Mark the stressed syllable in each word.

PERSON	VERB	CRIME
burglar thief robber	*'burgle* – _____	_____ _____ _____

3   Complete the sentences. Use one of the words above.
1 Someone _____ their house while they were on holiday.
2 They planned to _____ a bank.
3 The problem of car _____ is getting worse.

4   Complete these sentences with the correct form of the words in the box.

prison   arrest   steal   commit   thief

Police Constable Roberts heard the sound of footsteps. He went quietly into the house. Roberts hoped to _____ the burglar while he was _____ the crime. As Roberts got to the stairs, he jumped on the man. Roberts was horrified to see that the man was the judge who last week sent a _____ to _____ for six months because he _____ a box of chocolates.

5   Work in groups. Put the pictures on the right in the correct order. Write the story. Start like this:
First, he broke a window and ...

USE AND REVIEW

Sandra Helen Steven Rebecca Mark

1 Work with a partner.

STUDENT A

Look at page 126.

STUDENT B

Look at the picture above. You are going to ask your partner five questions about the people. First write your questions. Example:

Is Sandra taller than Helen?

a) Show your partner your picture. Ask him/her your questions.

b) Compare the people in the two pictures. Example:

I think Helen is the most attractive.

2 Choose one of the people in your picture.

a) Which hobby do you think he/she does?

b) Imagine you are the person in the picture. Tell your partner about your hobby. Why do you like it? Don't say who you are.

c) Your partner must guess who you are.

Language reference

1 Would

FORM

Positive		
I / You / We / He / She / They **'d (would)**		like to be rich.
Negative		
I / You / We / He / She / They	**wouldn't (would not)**	like to be rich.
Question		
Would	I / you / we / he / she / they	like to be rich?

USE

a) for requests (**Would** *you like a drink?*)
b) to express a wish (*I***'d** *like to go to the cinema.*)
c) when we imagine situations that are not likely to happen (*I***'d** *spend my perfect holiday on a luxury ship.*)

2 The Second Conditional

FORM

If + past form, *would* (*'d*) + base form of verb

Positive
If I **found** *£20, I* **would keep** *it.*
Negative
If I **found** *£20, I* **wouldn't keep** *it.*   *If I* **didn't speak** *French, I* **wouldn't understand**.
Question
If you **found** *£20,* **would** *you* **keep** *it?*   *What* **would** *you* **do** *if you* **found** *£20?*
Short answer
If you **found** *£20,* **would** *you* **keep** *it?*   *Yes, I* **would**. / *No, I* **wouldn't**.

There is usually a comma after the *if*-clause and before the main clause (*If I thought he looked terrible***,** *I would …)* The *if* part of the sentence can come second and then there isn't a comma before *if*.

I wouldn't tell him **if** *I thought he looked terrible.*

USE

We use the Second Conditional when we imagine situations that are unlikely or impossible in the present or the future.

If I found £20 … (But I haven't and it is unlikely.)
If I were you … (But I'm not. It's impossible.)

We use past verb forms after *if* to show that a situation is imaginary. We are not talking about past time.

•Love is all around•

USE YOUR ENGLISH

Finding the way

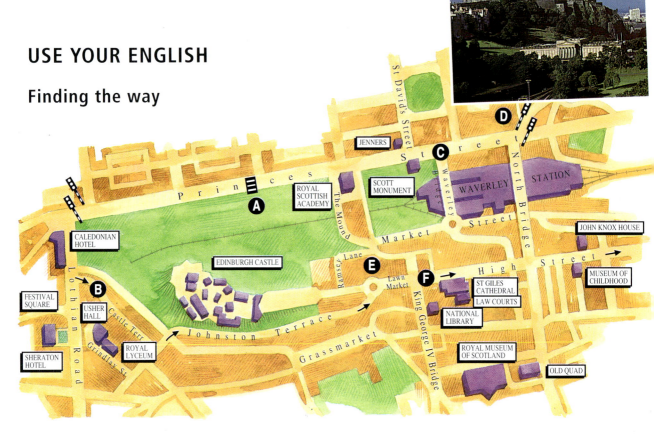

1 Look at this map of Central Edinburgh.

a) Can you find:

1 some traffic lights   4 a crossroads
2 a T-junction   5 a one-way street
3 a pedestrian crossing   6 a roundabout

b) Where are they? Match A with B.

A
1 The Museum of Childhood
2 Waverley Station
3 Jenners
4 St Giles Cathedral
5 The Old Quad
6 The Law Courts

B
a) on the corner of Princes Street and St David's Street
b) behind St Giles Cathedral
c) opposite John Knox House
d) next to the Royal Museum of Scotland
e) between Waverley Bridge and North Bridge
f) in front of the Law Courts

2 [🔲 13.1] Penny has invited Carl to a concert. She is giving him directions on the telephone.

a) Listen and follow Penny's directions on the map. Where is the concert hall?

b) Listen again and complete these sentences.

1 Turn _____ and _____ until you get to Princes Street.
2 _____ and walk _____ Princes Street for about fifteen minutes.
3 Go _____ the Royal Scottish Academy.
4 You'll see the Castle and the Mound _____.
5 When you get to the end of Princes Street, _____ again _____ Lothian Road.
6 Walk _____ Lothian Road.

3 Work with a partner. Choose a place on the map of Edinburgh. Don't tell your partner the name of the place. Give your partner directions from Waverley Station.

SKILLS

Listening

1 Read the words on the right. They are of part of a song called 'Love is all around'. The words in italics are wrong.

a) Replace the wrong words with one of the words in the box.

| toes | love | feel | come on | everywhere |

b) [🔲 13.2] Listen and check your answers.

2 [🔲 13.3] Listen and complete the song.

3 Answer these questions.

1 Is he sure she loves him?
2 What do you think they promised?

4 Which words rhyme with these words? Example: grows (line 4) *toes*.

go (line 6), depend (line 16), bed (line 18), you (line 22)

> 1 I *hear* it in my fingers
>   I *hear* it in my *nose*.
>   Well, love is all around me
>   and so the feeling grows.
> 5 It's written on the wind,
>   It's *nowhere* I go.
>   So if you really *hate* me
>   *Go away* and let it show.

> You know I love you,
> 10 I _____ will.
>   My mind's made up
>   By the way that I _____.
>   There's no beginning,
>   There'll be no _____
> 15 'Cos on my love, you can
>   depend.

>   I see your face before me,
>   As I lay on my _____.
>   I kind of get to thinking,
> 20 Of all the things you _____.
>   You gave your promise to me,
>   And I gave mine to _____.
>   I need someone beside me,
>   In everything I _____.

Reading and speaking

1 What does the word 'romantic' mean to you?

2 Read this extract from a survey on monogamy and answer the questions.

1 Some people think that staying married is very difficult. Who think this, younger people or older people?
2 Is it better to be romantic or unromantic if you want to stay married?

3 Work with a partner. Read about these people's ideas and answer the questions.

> You can't be romantic these days. Everybody is too busy working.

> We make sure we have a romantic holiday on a boat every year.

1 What different ways are there of being romantic?
2 Is it important for young people and old people to be romantic? Why/Why not?
3 What advice would you give to a couple who have been married for fifteen years and who want to be romantic?

Last week we interviewed 1000 people for our survey on monogamy. One in five people said, 'Monogamy is unnatural.' A quarter of the people said, 'Monogamy was all right twenty years ago but now it's old-fashioned.' And it wasn't the younger people who said that but those in their late twenties and older. They've tried to be together 'for always'. But for a lot of them it didn't work.

Nearly three-quarters of the people dreamed about marriage when they were children. They dreamt that they would marry and live with the same person for the rest of their lives. But often the most romantic people have broken marriages. And those who are most happily married generally didn't have dreams about their future when they were children.

(from *New Woman*)

Writing: reference words

1   What do the words in italics below refer to in the article on monogamy on page 79?

1 but now *it's* old-fashioned. (line 7)
2 the younger people who said *that* ... (line 9)
3 But for a lot of *them* it didn't work. (line 12)
4 *Those* who are most happily ... (line 21)

2   Complete these sentences. Do not repeat words from the first sentence.

1 I like French films. I like *them* a lot.
2 A: What do you think of *Hamlet*?
  B: I've never seen _____.
3 I like those jeans over there. They're better than _____ you're wearing.
4 A: Pam's just got married.
  B: Who told you _____?
5 A: I saw Jim today.
  B: Where did you see _____?
6 A: A woman called for you today.
  B: What was _____ name?

GRAMMAR

Defining relative clauses: *who, which, that, where*

1   Tick (✓) the boxes you agree with and add sentences of your own.

Likes and dislikes

1 *What kind of people do you like?*

a) I like people who (that)
   show their feelings ☐   laugh a lot ☐   give a lot of presents ☐
   I like people _____

b) I am jealous of people who (that)
   can eat anything and stay slim ☐   always look wonderful ☐
   understand computers ☐
   I am jealous of people _____

c) I don't like people who (that)
   hurt animals ☐   drive badly ☐   eat garlic ☐
   I don't like people _____

2 *What kind of things do you like?*
   (Examples: cars, animals, films)

I like trains which (that) run on time. ☐
I don't like dogs which (that) bark a lot. ☐
I like/don't like _____

3 *What kind of places do you like?*
   (Examples: hotels, airports)

I like shops where the assistants are polite. ☐
I don't like restaurants where they play music. ☐
I like/don't like _____

2   When we want to add information and make it clear which person, thing or place we are talking about we use:

1 _____ (or *that*) for people.   3 _____ for places.
2 _____ (or *that*) for things.

Complete these sentences with *who, which, that,* or *where*.

1 Have you been back to the town _____ you were born?
2 She's the kind of person _____ likes to go to parties.
3 Who took the bag _____ was on the table?
4 A vegetarian is someone _____ doesn't eat meat.
5 That is the horse _____ won the race.

Using your grammar

1   Work in groups. Ask each other the questions from the questionnaire. Example:
Do you like people who show their feelings?

Write down the answers. Report back to the class.

2   Complete these sentences

1 The perfect parent is someone who ...
2 My ideal room is a place where ...
3 Computers are things which ...
4 A good host is someone who ...

3   These are meanings of some difficult words from units 1–12. Is each sentence *True* (T) or *False* (F)?

1 A chemist's is a place where you buy books.
2 A cardigan is like a jacket which keeps you warm.
3 A greengrocer is someone who sells stamps.
4 10 Downing Street is the place where the President of the USA lives.
5 A model is someone who wears new clothes at shows.
6 A platform is a place where you get on a plane.
7 A shoplifter is someone who builds houses.
8 Slippers are shoes which people wear in the house.

Adjectives: word order

1   Read these sentences.
I like men with large, round, brown eyes who wear nice clothes.
A wallet is a small, flat, leather case for paper money.

SIZE	SHAPE	COLOUR	MATERIAL
large	round	brown	
small	flat		leather

2   Put the adjective in brackets in the correct place. Example:
a square box (wooden)   *a square wooden box*

1 a long woollen scarf (grey)
2 a pointed thing (large)
3 a dark road (long)
4 a big cat (white)

(We) use a ... for ...-ing

1   Match the words with the pictures.

1 a vacuum cleaner
2 a buggy
3 a corkscrew
4 scissors
5 glue
6 a blanket
7 a purse

2   What do we use the things in Exercise 1 for? Example:
*We **use** a vacuum cleaner **for** cleaning carpets.*

Using your grammar

Work with a partner. Describe one of the things below to your partner. He/She must guess which thing you are describing.

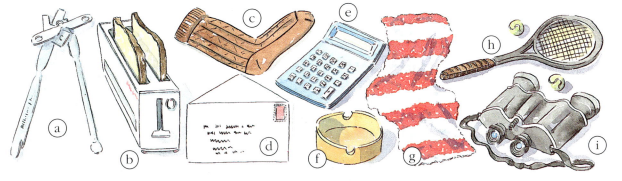

VOCABULARY

Describing people

1 [📼 13.4]   Listen. Four people are trying to find their friends.

a) Match the pictures of the friends with the conversations.

b) Listen again. Write the expressions which describe the friends. Make two lists: 1 Expressions with *is* (*He / She is quite tall*); 2 Expressions with *has (got)* (*He / She has (got) long, black hair*).

c) Add more expressions to each list. Example: opposites like *short blond hair*.

d) In these sentences, the words in *italics* are not appropriate. Replace the word in *italics* with one of the words in brackets.

1 She's lovely and *skinny*. (bony, slim)
2 Rob's a very *pretty* man. (handsome, beautiful)
3 Lucy is very *high*. (tall, great) She's not *middle-height*. (medium, average height)

The correct words are in the conversations in Exercise 1a). Listen again and check.

2   We can use the adjectives in the box on the right to describe people's personalities. Make three lists: 1 Good; 2 Bad; 3 Not

Add other words to each list.

lazy	clever	tidy
sociable	bad-tempered	
lively	patient	mean
cheerful	talkative	shy

Relationships

Read Matthew's letter to an old friend who lives in the USA. They haven't seen each other for many years. Complete the sentences with the correct form of the verbs in the box. Use a dictionary to help you.

go out together	fall in love
get married	be fond of
get divorced	get pregnant

I _____ Laura at school but I didn't really fancy her until we met at a dance several years later. The next day I took her to the cinema. That was the day we first kissed and _____. It was very romantic. We _____ for about a year before we _____ and decided to have a baby. Soon afterwards Laura _____ and we had a baby boy we called James. We both adored him. Unfortunately that was the beginning of our problems. We argued about everything. Two years later we _____ but we've stayed good friends. We still see each other every week and take James out together.

Using your vocabulary

Read the two lists on the right.

a) Imagine **your** ideal partner. Make two similar lists.
b) Work with a partner. Compare your lists.

I want someone who
• is kind
• wears nice clothes
• has got blue eyes
I don't want someone who
• is bad-tempered
• has a very long beard

USE AND REVIEW

1 Read this extract from a magazine article. Why was Suzanne brave?

Suzanne Daniel, a hospital secretary, was out shopping last week. She was walking along the street when a shop assistant screamed. A thief ran out of a shop with a heavy cash register.

Suzanne and the thief came face to face. She tried to stop the thief but he pushed past her. Then she ran after him down the street and tried to stop him getting into his car. Furious, the thief threw the cash register at her and ran away.

2 What would you do in these situations? Use the ideas in brackets.

1 You are walking down a street and you see a thief running out of a shop with a cash register. (*If I saw ..., try to stop / run away / phone the police / do nothing*)
2 You see someone shoplifting. (*tell assistant / speak to the person / do nothing*)
3 You hear someone in your house in the night. (*phone police / get a gun / hide*)
4 You see smoke coming from inside a house. (*phone fire station / go and look*)

3 Complete these sentences.

1 You would go to prison in my country if ...
2 If I had 10 children, ...
3 You would feel better if ...
4 If I couldn't sleep for three days, ...
5 Would you give me a kiss if ...?

4 What nouns, verbs or adjectives do you associate with *police, kill* and *steal?* There are example words in the box. Add more words.

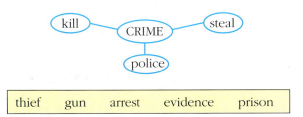

| thief | gun | arrest | evidence | prison |

Language reference

1 Defining relative clauses

Who, which, that, where are relative pronouns. We use them to link ideas, add information and make it clear which person, thing or place we are talking about.

a) *who* or *that*

We use *who* (or sometimes *that*) for a person or people.
  *I like people **who (that)** listen.*
  *I don't like people **who (that)** talk all the time.*
  *She is the doctor **who (that)** lives next door.*

b) *which* or *that*

We use *which* or *that* for things.
  *I'm talking about a car **which (that)** uses very little petrol.*

c) *where*

We use *where* for places.
  *A library is a place **where** you borrow books.*

Note that there is no comma before a defining relative clause.

2 Adjectives: word order

(See page 81.)

3 *(We) use a ... for ...-ing*

  *What do you **use** this **for**?*
  *I **use** it **for** clean**ing** the carpet.*

• A real fan •

I've just won the competition!

USE YOUR ENGLISH

Saying the right thing

1   Work with a partner. What would you say in answer to the people on the right? Choose the best answer, a), b) or c).

1 a) Good luck!   b) Hard luck!   c) Well done!
2 a) Oh! What a pity!   b) I don't care.   c) Not at all, don't mention it.
3 a) Yes, it's all right.   b) Sorry!   c) That's a good idea.
4 a) That's no good.   b) Oh, I **am** sorry!   c) Better luck next time.

2   Complete these conversations.

a) Choose the best answer, a), b) or c).

I'm sorry I can't come to your party.

1 PAM: Hi, Sue. Guess what?   PAM: I'm having a baby in July.
  SUE: What?   SUE: Oh, _____.

   a) Well done!   b) Congratulations!   c) It'll be all right.

2 SHOP ASSISTANT ONE: I'll get one for you. I won't be a second.
   RICHARD: That's OK.
   SHOP ASSISTANT TWO: Can I help you?
   RICHARD: _____.

   a) No, I'm being served, thanks.   b) Yes, I hope so.
   c) Certainly.

Quiet!

b) [🖭 14.1]   Listen and check your answers.

3   Work with a partner. You have been at a friend's house for the weekend. These sentences are from your conversation on Sunday evening.

a) Put the conversation in the correct order.

- Well, it's time to go. We've had a great time. Thanks for everything.   ☑
- Sure. Bye. Look after yourself.   ☐
- Next time you must come to us.   ☐
- Yes, we'd love to. Have a safe journey. Don't forget to write.   ☐
- Not at all. We've enjoyed having you here.   ☐

My brother's not well.

b) [🖭 14.2]   Listen and check your answers.

SKILLS

Reading

People who 'follow' famous people are called 'fans'. Read these articles on the right about two fans, Saf and Ruth. Saf is a fan of Geroge Michael. Ruth is a fan of Barbra Streisand.

a) Work with a partner and answer these questions.

   1 Saf is obsessed (he thinks about the singer most of the time). How do you know?

   2 How do you know Ruth is obsessed?

   3 How are Saf and Ruth different?

b) Work in two groups.

GROUP A

Read the article about Saf again and write questions for these answers. Example: He owns a newsagent's shop. *What does Saf do?*

   1 CDs and copies of George's suits.

   2 In January.

   3 Ten years ago.

   4 On TV.

GROUP B

Read the article about Ruth again and write questions for these answers. Example: She is going to hear Barbra sing. *What is Ruth going to do next week?*

   1 Three months ago.

   2 Thousands and thousands of pounds.

   3 Yes, she feels she is an old friend now.

   4 A lot.

c) Work with a partner from the other group. Check your partner's questions.

I'm a real fan

SAF SATHI, 25, is known as 'George' in the newsagent's shop he owns in Kent, because of his obsession with the singer George
5 Michael.

Saf spends his life trying to be better than George Michael's other fans. He earns £400 a week. Out of this £400 he buys every
10 new Michael CD (at £12 each) and copies of George Michael's suits (at £300 each). His wife, Savita, is expecting a baby in January: he would like to name it
15 'Michael' if it's a boy.

'I've got all his albums on tape and CD. I know exactly what he's doing. I don't miss a thing,' Saf says.

20 Saf's obsession started about ten years ago when George Michael was in the pop group *Wham!* 'He's so smart. His clothes, his look, the way he is
25 different from the others.'

Saf's dream is to be George Michael. Already well-known for copying his idol, he is now trying to get work on TV as a
30 George Michael lookalike.

Next week Ruth Davison will spend 10 per cent of her annual salary. She is
35 going to hear Barbra Streisand sing. Miss Davison, an office clerk, has bought seats for all four of Barbra Streisand's concerts in London, at £260 a
40 ticket.

However, that is not as much as she spent on flying to Las Vegas to see Streisand's $1,000-a-ticket show three months
45 ago. It is also not as much as she spent on a Beverly Hills show that she flew to California for. It was there that Miss Davison, 32, met and spoke to Streisand.
50 'I said I'd come all the way from England. She said "Oh, good," and smiled nicely. That made it worth the money.'

Most of Streisand's fans are
55 not rich. Many, like Miss Davison, are prepared to spend all their savings to see one of the last superstars in the world.

'I can't think of anything I
60 would rather spend my money

on,' says Miss Davison. 'I've spent thousands and thousands of pounds over the years. Any spare money I've got goes on
65 Barbra. No one else can sing like her. It touches you deep inside and makes you want to get to know her. I feel I know her well now. I feel she is an old
70 friend.

'I can feel her feelings. I believe she worries a lot and I don't think she's very confident. But she's done a lot
75 for women. She has made it possible for women to become film directors. She was one of the very first.'

(from *The Daily Telegraph* and *The Independent on Sunday*)

Vocabulary

1 Match the words from the articles about Saf and Ruth in A with their meanings in B.

A	B
1 miss (line 18)	a) *adj* for one year
2 annual (line 34)	b) *adj* sure of yourself
3 spare (line 64)	c) *v* fail to get
4 confident (line 74)	d) *adj* extra

2 Complete these sentences with the correct form of one of the words from Exercise 1.

1 I'm nervous. I don't feel very _____.
2 What's your _____ salary?
3 Have you got a _____ pen I could borrow?
4 We arrived at the station late and _____ the train.

Writing

Adverbials in sentences

> a) Adverbials of manner come after the object or after the verb if there is no object.
> *Barbra smiled at her **nicely**.*
> b) Adverbials of time usually come at the end or sometimes at the beginning of a sentence.
> *He came to see me **last week**.*
> ***Last week** he came to see me.*
> c) Adverbials of place usually go at the end of a sentence.
> *We walked slowly **into town**.*
> d) See page 17 for frequency adverbs.

Put these words in order.

1 speaks / he / English / well
2 quickly / ran / road / he / the / down
3 early / went / she / bed / night / last / to
4 her / to / listens / always / he / carefully

GRAMMAR

Used to

1 The writer Margaret Forster is talking about being fifty.

I haven't changed my idea of a good time very much over the years. I used to enjoy staying in with a new novel and a really good apple, and now I enjoy staying in with a new novel and a glass of wine.

I used to behave very badly in my twenties. I remember once I screamed in the middle of Oxford Street and all the cars suddenly stopped. In my thirties I was too tired to find the energy to scream.

It used to be very difficult to write. I wanted to be a mother, a writer and a wife and do everything myself. Now I can write all day if I want to.

(from *Male and Femail)*

1 When Margaret stayed at home in the past, what did she do?
2 When she stays at home now, what does she do?
3 What was she like in her twenties and her thirties?
4 Did she often use to scream in the middle of Oxford Street?
5 Was it difficult for her to write in the past?
6 Is it difficult for her to write now?

2 Look at the *Language reference* on page 89 for information about *used to*.

a) Complete these sentences with the Past Simple or *used to*. In one sentence both verb forms are possible. Which one?

1 Yesterday morning I *(have)* _____ toast for breakfast.
2 When I was young I *(like)* _____ toast.

b) Complete these sentences with *used to* and the base form of a verb.

1 I _____ out a lot but now I stay in more.
2 When Tony was younger he _____ sweets but he doesn't like them now.
3 Megan _____ in France but now she lives in Wales.
4 Children _____ books but now they play computer games.

3 [🖭 14.3]   Listen to these sentences and mark the stressed words. Example: *We 'used to 'swim in the 'sea.*

1 I used to wear short skirts.
2 He used to drive fast cars.
3 We used to listen to the radio.
4 I used to be very unhappy.
5 She used to eat meat but now she's a vegetarian.

4 Make sentences with *used to* from these pictures and words. Example:
People used to travel by boat but now they travel by plane.

1 I/live Rio/Paris 2 Pete/poor/rich 3 Angie/ride/drive

Question tags

1 Read about tonight's TV programmes. What would you like to watch?

6.00 WILDLIFE ON ONE
(repeat) Elephants in India.

6.30 FILM: STAR TREK V: THE FINAL FRONTIER
N
(1989) Vulcan kidnaps three people. A Klingon warship goes to help. Stars William Shatner.

8.10 PANORAMA
A day in the life of a nurse in modern Britain.

9.00 NEWS & WEATHER

9.30 HEADHUNTERS
T
New drama in the world of big business. Stars James Fox and Francesca Annis.

10.20 RORY BREMNER
N T
Successful comedian gives his ideas about love.

11.00 LATER WITH JOOLS HOLLAND
N
Chat and music with Sting and reggae from Sly and Robbie.

2 [14.4] Nikki and Tom are talking about tonight's TV.

a) Listen. Which programmes does Nikki like? Which programmes does Tom like?

b) Complete the sentences.

1 He's a good actor, _____?
2 It wasn't very good last week, _____?
3 You still like Sting, _____?
4 We've seen it, _____?
5 You liked him last time, _____?
6 Let's watch that, _____?

c) [14.5] Listen and check your answers. Look at the *Language reference* on page 89 for information about question tags.

Using your grammar

Used to

Work with a partner. Tell him/her about the changes in your life over the years. Talk about things like:

- daily routine
- hobbies
- clothes
- personality
- travel
- likes/dislikes
- sports
- food

Question tags

Work with a partner. Find out about Keanu Reeves.

STUDENT A
Look at page 126.

STUDENT B
Read this article.

KEANU REEVES

was born in Beirut in 1965. His mother is English and his father is Chinese-Hawaiian. When he was young he wanted to be a racing driver. Keanu began acting when he was 18. He has played in the films *Dracula* and *Much Ado About Nothing*. Keanu loves riding motorbikes. He has got a 1974 Norton.

You and your partner both have information about Keanu Reeves. Most of the information is the same, but you've got some information which your partner hasn't got. Use question tags to check and find the extra information. Example:
A: *He was born in 1965, wasn't he?*
B: *Yes, he was.*

VOCABULARY

Entertainment

1 We use these things in home entertainment. Match the words in the box with the pictures.

| video recorder CDs loudspeaker cassette |
| video tapes batteries TV screen headphones |
| stereo system microphone |

2 We use the words in the box for other kinds of entertainment.

| exhibition screen interval performance |
| front row audience to book stage to clap |
| sculpture to buy a programme drawing |

Make three lists with the words in the box for: 1 A pop concert; 2 An art gallery; 3 A cinema. Use a dictionary to help you.

3 Where would you hear these sentences? Match the sentences in A with the places in B.

A
1 'I like it when the clowns throw water at each other.'
2 'It's so cruel! I hate to see the animals locked up.'
3 'Everything here is so old, Dad!'
4 'How much money have you lost?'

B
a) a museum
b) a casino
c) a circus
d) a zoo

4 Look at the puzzle. Find the word for someone who:

1 acts (a _____)
2 plays funny parts on TV or in a film (c _____)
3 directs a play or a film (d _____)
4 plays a musical instrument in public (m _____)
5 directs an orchestra (c _____)
6 writes a book (a _____)
7 creates works of art (a _____)
8 writes music (c _____)

```
F L G U A D K I A T J
C O N D U C T O R P G
D F A C T O R Z T Y J
I M V B H J E S I P L
R F P C O M P O S E R
E P W N R T Z X T Y M
C U Y C O M E D I A N
T O W Q A Z V F H J L
O M U S I C I A N R W
R T W A O G F D K J U
```

Using your vocabulary

Work with a partner. Talk about something you have watched, heard or read recently. Use some of the adjectives from the box. Ask and answer questions like:

What was the title? Who directed, sang or wrote it? What was it about? What was your opinion of it?

| interesting exciting amusing boring relaxing |
| shocking frightening depressing |

USE AND REVIEW

1 Work in groups. Complete these sentences with *who*, *which* or *where* and give the answer. The group with all the correct answers wins.
Example:
A person who paints pictures is a painter.

1 The place _____ you catch a train is a _____.
2 A person _____ looks after sick people in hospital is a _____.
3 A thing _____ you imagine when you are asleep is a _____.
4 A person _____ cuts your hair is a _____.
5 A long thin animal without legs _____ eats other animals is a _____.
6 A place _____ you buy medicine is a _____.
7 A person _____ writes for a newspaper is a _____.

2 Work with a partner.

STUDENT A
Look at page 127.

a) STUDENT B
You and your partner have similar pictures. Ask questions and find ten differences. Don't look at your partner's picture and don't show him/her your picture.

b) Now look at your partner's picture and answer these questions.

1 What does the woman look like?
2 What kind of person do you think she is?
3 Where is she?
4 What is happening in the picture?

Language reference

1 Used to

FORM

Used to + base form of the verb

Positive and negative			
I / You / We	**used to**	**like**	wine.
They / He / She	**didn't use to**	**drive**	fast cars.
Question			
Did you **use to smoke**?		Yes, I **did**. / No, I **didn't**.	
How many cigarettes **did** you **use to smoke**?			

USE

Used to can express a past situation which has finished or changed.
  I **used to like** *jazz but now I like rock.*
  I **used to go** *to jazz clubs every week.*
We do not need to use a time expression with *used to*. In the above examples we can also use the Past Simple with a time expression.
  I **liked** *jazz* **when I was younger** *but now I like rock.*
  I **went** *to jazz clubs* **when I was at college**.
We cannot use *used to* when something happened only once:
  I went to a rock concert last night. (NOT ~~used to go~~)

2 Question tags

FORM

Positive sentence + negative tag.
  They're happy, **aren't they**?
Negative sentence + positive tag.
  She **isn't** *right,* **is she**?
In sentences with *is/ are* or with an auxiliary *doesn't/ don't, have/ has, can/ should* we make the tag with *is/ are* or the auxiliary.
  There's nothing left, **is** *there?*
  Peter **doesn't** *like you,* **does** *he?*
  She **hasn't** *finished,* **has** *she?*
In sentences without an auxiliary we make the tag with *do/ does/ did.*
  He likes you, **doesn't** *he?*
  You went to New York, **didn't** *you?*
Note there are two exceptions.
  I'm late, **aren't** *I?*
  Let's go out, **shall** *we?*

USE

We use question tags when we think the other person agrees with us or we want the other person to agree with us. Our voices usually go down at the end of question tags.

School rules

USE YOUR ENGLISH

Changing money

1   Carlos is a student. He has just arrived from Argentina for a week's holiday in Britain. What has he got in his wallet?

1 How much sterling can you see?
2 How can he get sterling when he has no more cash?

2   Carlos is changing a traveller's cheque at a bank.

a) Read this conversation and complete the sentences.

BANK CLERK: Yes, sir?
CARLOS: Can I _____ a traveller's cheque for $100?
BANK CLERK: Sure. _____ at the top, please. Can I see your passport?

CARLOS: What's the _____ rate at the moment?
BANK CLERK: $1.41 to the pound. So that's £70. How would you _____ the money?
CARLOS: Three twenties and a ten, please.

b) [15.1]   Listen and check your answers.
c) Work with a partner and practise the conversation.

3   Work with a partner. Look at the list of £ exchange rates. Change the sums of money below (cash or traveller's cheques) into sterling. Take turns to be the bank clerk and the customer.

- seventy five Cyprus pounds
- one thousand five hundred Japanese yen
- three hundred Swiss francs
- 500 Austrian schillings
- two hundred Brazilian reals

4   Look at the pictures. Carlos is buying a coat in a shop.

a) What do you think Carlos and the shop assistant are saying?
b) Write a conversation beginning:

CARLOS: How much ... ?

Tourist rates

Austrian schilling	16.40
Brazilian real	1.36
Cyprus pound	0.73
French franc	7.96
German mark	2.35
Greek drachma	358.00
Italian lire	2755.00
Japanese yen	156.93
Spanish peseta	194.00
Swiss franc	1.97
US dollar	1.41

SKILLS

Reading and speaking

Work with a partner. Read about a school in England and answer the questions.

1 What are the differences between this school and your school?
2 What is/was a school day like in your school? (Example: *The day started at ...*)
3 Think about schools in your country. Make a list of rules (Example: *You have to wear a uniform. No fighting.*) and punishments (Example: *Staying after school.*)

THE KING'S SCHOOL, ELY

The school day begins at 8.50 am. Children have to be at school by 8.40 am and the day ends at 4.00 pm. There are classes on Saturdays.

All pupils have lunch at school.

All children have to wear school uniform in the day time. The uniform is simple and inexpensive.

Listening and speaking

1   Look at the photos. Guess which school has more rules.

2 [🖭 15.2]   Karen, from the USA, and Rie, from Japan, are fifteen. At the moment they are at the King's School in Ely, England. Listen to them talking about schools in their countries. In which country do the pupils spend more time at school?

3   Work in groups.

[🖭 15.3] GROUP A, listen to Karen.

[🖭 15.4] GROUP B, listen to Rie.

Look at the list on the right. What rules and punishments do you hear?

4   Work with a partner from the other group.

a) Compare your information. Answer these questions.

   1 Which school has more rules?
   2 What do students in the American school do when their teachers ask them to stay in the classroom at lunchtime?
   3 How do Karen's and Rie's schools in their countries compare with their school in England?
   4 What is the difference between modern and traditional school uniforms in Japan?

b) Ask your partner about his/her school. Use these words to help you: *like school? memories? your first day? how old? good / bad things about schools in your country?*

RULES

She has to
• wear a school uniform
• study very hard

She mustn't
• take drugs
• wear her school uniform to town
• smoke
• fight
• wear a hat

In her school she can
• talk in class
• do what she likes
• wear what she likes
• not go to classes

PUNISHMENTS

The teachers sometimes
• call the police *(the cops)*
• ask students to stay after school
• phone the pupils' parents

Vocabulary

Karen uses the informal word *cops* to talk about 'the police'. Match the informal words in italics with the words in the box. Use a dictionary to help you.

employer	very good
want wait	children

1 I'm taking the *kids* to the zoo.
2 Do you *fancy* a drink?
3 *Hang on* a minute.
4 He asked his *boss* for more money.
5 We're *great* friends.

Writing: linking words

> Note where the linking words come in a sentence.
>
> **CONTRAST**
> a) School finishes at 4 **but** we can't go home until 7. (middle)
> b) **Although** school finishes at 4, we can't go home until 7.
> We can't go home until 7, **although** school finishes at 4. (beginning or middle)
> c) School finishes at 4. **However**, we can't go home until 7. (beginning)
>
> **ADDITION**
> a) Karen goes to school in England. Rie goes to school in England, **too**. (end)
> b) Karen goes to school in England. Rie **also** goes to school in England. (She is **also** studying in England.) (before the main verb but after verbs like be, have, can)

Join these sentences with linking words. Change the order of the words if necessary.

1 The actors were very good. I didn't like the film very much.
2 I'll buy this bag. I'll buy these shoes.
3 My car is old. It runs very well.

GRAMMAR

Quantity

Mrs Todd

Some-, any-, no-, every- words

1 Mrs Todd is talking about modern life.

a) Look at the words in italics. Which one do you think is correct?

'These days *everyone/someone* is very busy. There's not enough time for *something/anything*. *Someone/No one* stops to talk to you. I hate it.'

b) [🔊 15.5] Listen and check your answers.
c) Which correct answer in a) means:
• no people?
• all people?
d) In negative sentences do we use *something* or *anything*? (See page 41 for the difference between *some* and *any*.)

2 Complete the sentences. Use one of the words in the box:

PEOPLE			THINGS		
some-/any- no/every-	+	one	some-/any- no-/every-	+	thing

1 I've got *something* for you. I hope you like it.
2 Please close your eyes. I don't want _____ to look.
3 There's _____ in the box. It's empty.
4 There's _____ at home. Where have they gone? _____'s out.
5 I can't do _____ right. _____ I say is wrong.
6 I've never met _____ as intelligent as you.
7 There's _____ on the phone for you.
8 The office is empty. Where is _____?

Sarah

Mr Parsons

Too and very

> It's **very** warm today. It's great. Let's go out.
> It's **too** warm today to go out. Let's stay in.
>
> Too means 'more than is good'.

3 Mr Parsons is talking about modern houses.

a) Complete his sentences with *too* or *very* .

'I like modern houses. I moved into one last year. It's _____ nice. I didn't like my old house. It was _____ big for me. The one I live in now is _____ small but it's just right for me. I'm _____ old to live in a big house.'

b) [📼 15.6] Listen and check your answers.

4 Make sentences about these pictures using *too*.

old/swimming   2 tired/go out   3 ill/get up   4 expensive/buy

5 Join these sentences using *very* or *too*.

1 He is young. He can't get married.
2 It's dark. You can't see the road.
3 This programme is interesting. It is interesting for children.
4 My coffee is hot. I can't drink it.

Too much and too many

6 Read these sentences.

*I ate **too much** food last night. I feel ill this morning. There are **too many** students in the class. One of them is going to another class.*

Match the words in the box with *too much* or *too many*. (See page 41, for the difference between *much* and *many*.)

> people   time   houses
> salt   trees   money

7 Sarah is talking about how she relaxes.

a) Complete her sentences with *too much* or *too many*.

'Everyone works very hard these days. During the week I can't relax. I have _____ to do. So on Saturdays I like to find something to read and take a long deep bath. I might watch TV but these days I think there are _____ game shows on. I don't like them.'

b) [📼 15.7] Listen and check your answers.

8 Make sentences using *too much* or *too many*. Example: Sorry / can't come. People to see.
I'm sorry I can't come. I've got too many people to see.

1 Can't buy / house. Costs / money.
2 You've got / furniture / clothes. Sell some.
3 Can't see. People in front of me.
4 Spend / time watching TV.
5 Can't eat this cake. Sugar.

VOCABULARY

Education

1   Look at the pictures on the right.

a)   Match the school subjects with the pictures.

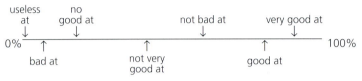

> languages   science   art   IT (information technology)

b)   Make a list of other school subjects. Examples: *maths, history.*
c)   Which subjects are/were you:

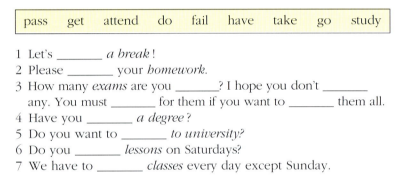

d)   Which subjects do/did you enjoy most?

2   The verbs in the box often go with the nouns in italics.
Complete the sentences with the correct form of the verbs.
Sometimes more than one answer is possible.

> pass   get   attend   do   fail   have   take   go   study

1 Let's _____ *a break* !
2 Please _____ your *homework.*
3 How many *exams* are you _____? I hope you don't _____
  any. You must _____ for them if you want to _____ them all.
4 Have you _____ *a degree* ?
5 Do you want to _____ *to university*?
6 Do you _____ *lessons* on Saturdays?
7 We have to _____ *classes* every day except Sunday.

Je m'appelle
Marie

Using your vocabulary

1   Work in groups. Which sentences do you agree with? Why?
Number the sentences 1 to 8. (1 = you agree with this sentence
the most.)

1 Schools should teach more practical subjects.
  (Examples: *cooking, typing.*)
2 Music and art should be extra classes.
3 There shouldn't be sports in school time.
4 There shouldn't be school uniforms.
5 Parents should help in the school.

6 We should have our education when we are
  adults, not when we are children.
7 Parents should educate their children at home.
8 You learn more from going to work than going
  to university.

2   Compare these ideas. Which help you to learn best?
Example: *You learn more from your parents than from television.*

• books   • your friends   • television   • working   • school   • parents

USE AND REVIEW

1   There is one mistake in each sentence. Can you correct the mistakes?

1 Carly used to go to a Thai restaurant last night.
2 These days, I used to catch the bus at six o'clock every morning.
3 When he was younger he used to spending every Saturday in bed.
4 You haven't seen her, haven't you?
5 David likes tennis, likes he?

2   Can you do this crossword puzzle?

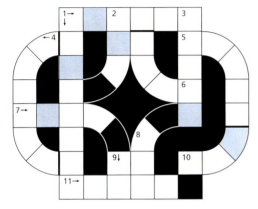

a) Follow the direction of the arrows and write answers. Use a dictionary if necessary.

1 → Somebody who writes books.
1 ↓ The people who watch a pop concert.
2 ↓ The in_____val in the middle of the concert lasts thirty minutes.
3 ↓ A: Let's go out.   B: All _____ then.
4 ← It happens every year. The event is _____.
5 → Let's go to the c_____ and have a good time. I always like the elephants.
6 ← A: Can I speak to Julie?
   B: _____ on a moment.
7 → A m_____m is a place where the public can look at interesting objects.
8 ↓ I am a big _____ of the Manchester United football team.
9 ↓ Leonardo da Vinci was a great _____tist.
10 → We took the children to the _____ to see the monkeys.
11 → She _____ £20,000 a year.

b) Put the letters in blue in the correct order to find an important grammar point (two words).

Language reference

1 *Some-*, *any-*, *no-*, *every-* words

FORM

The words *some*, *any*, *no* and *every* can join with the words *-one* and *-thing*. *(someone, everything)*.

USE

We use the words *someone, anyone, no one, everyone* for people *(one = person)*. We use the words *something, anything, nothing, everything* for things.

a) *Some-* words *(someone, something)*

Positive
   *I want you to meet **someone**.*
Offers and requests
   *Would you like **something** to drink?*
   *Could I have **something** to eat?*

b) *Any-* words *(anyone, anything)*

Questions
*Did you see **anyone**?*
Negatives
*I haven't done **anything** today.*

c) *No-* words *(no one, nothing)*

no one = no person
   *There's **no one** at home. They're all out.*
nothing = no thing
   *There's **nothing** in the room. It's empty.*

d) *Every-* words *(everyone, everything)*

everyone = all people
   ***Everyone**'s out. There's no one at home.*
everything = all things
   *The shop sells **everything** you need.*

2 *Very* or *too*?

too = more than is good, right or necessary.
   *It's **very** late. We must go.*
   *It's **too** late. We have missed the last bus.*
   *This coffee is **too** hot to drink.*

3 *Too much* or *too many*?

too much/too many = more (in quantity) than necessary
too much = before uncountable nouns.
   *We have **too much** milk.*
   *There's **too much** to do.*
too many = before countable nouns.
   *We have **too many** books.*
   *There are **too many** people.*

Have you heard the news?

USE YOUR ENGLISH

Saying sorry

1 What has happened in the photographs on the right?

a) In each of the pictures what does the other person say next? Choose one of these:

1 I'm awfully sorry. I didn't see you there.
2 Sorry. I had a very important business meeting.
3 I'm very sorry. I haven't got any more.
4 Sorry, but my watch stopped.

b) What does the first person answer? Choose one of these:

1 It doesn't matter. It's not your fault.
2 Oh, yes. You always say that.
3 That's all right. Don't worry.
4 I don't believe you.

c) [🔲 16.1] Listen. Were your guesses correct?

Where have you been?

For heaven's sake. Look what you are doing!

2 [🔲 16.2] The British use the word 'Sorry!' in many other situations. Listen to this conversation on the London Underground then put the pictures in the correct order. Listen again and complete the sentences.

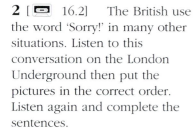

1 ANDY: You didn't —— me last night.
   NICOLA : —— ?
2 Oh, —— . Are you trying to —— —— ?
3 —— but this is —— —— date.

3 Work with a partner. Make conversations for these situations. Use 'sorry' where necessary.

1	2	3
STUDENT A You've broken a glass in a restaurant. Tell the waiter.	**STUDENT A** Invite B to a party.	**STUDENT A** Tell B you are cold.
STUDENT B You are the waiter. Be polite.	**STUDENT B** Refuse politely and give a reason.	**STUDENT B** You can't hear what A is saying. Ask him/her to repeat.

SKILLS

Reading and speaking

1 These pictures show two different newspaper stories. Which three pictures tell a story about a man who eats light bulbs and razor blades? What do you think the other story is about?

2 Work in two groups.

a) GROUP A: Read 'Call me Mother'.
GROUP B: Read 'Jim's dangerous life'.

b) Which of these sentences are *not* correct?

GROUP A

1 The old lady ...
a) arrived at the restaurant with the couple.
b) said the woman looked like her daughter.
c) hoped the woman would meet her daughter.
d) wanted the couple to pay for her.

2 The couple ...
a) wanted to talk to the old lady.
b) felt sorry for the old lady.
c) thought the lady was telling the truth.
d) asked why the lady's meal was not on the bill.

GROUP B

1 Jim Rose isn't paid for his work.
2 The police asked him to do a show.
3 The police thought he was drunk.
4 His mouth was full of wine.
5 Jim only eats one light bulb a day.
6 He ate a light bulb for a radio programme.
7 It hurt him immediately.
8 The doctors were angry when they found glass inside him.

3 Work with a partner from the other group. Tell your story in your own words. Use the pictures in Exercise 1 and the answers from Exercise 2.

CALL ME MOTHER

A friend and her husband were enjoying a romantic evening at an expensive restaurant when they saw an elderly lady. She was sitting all alone looking in their direction. They smiled back politely and the old lady went across to their table. 'I'm sorry to trouble you,' she began, trying not to cry, 'but you look like my daughter. She was killed last year and I do miss her terribly. I wonder if you would do something very kind for me?' The couple said yes.

'It would make me very happy if, just as I'm leaving, you would say, "Goodbye mum", and wave to me.'

'Certainly,' the couple replied. How could they possibly refuse? A few minutes later the old lady stood up to leave so the couple waved and said 'goodbye' as 'mum' walked out.

Then the couple asked for their bill. But after checking and rechecking, they called the manager because they thought the total was wrong.

'This £25 is for your mother's meal,' the manager told them. 'Before she left she said that her daughter would pay.'

Jim's dangerous life

It was not a good week for Jim Rose, an unusual man who eats razor blades and light bulbs and breathes fire for a living.

On Monday Rose was driving from London to Amsterdam when he was stopped by police and breathalysed. Rose does not drink alcohol. However, he had put so much alcohol in his mouth when he was breathing fire that the breathalyser almost blew up. He had to pay £250.

Then for a radio programme, Rose ate a light bulb (his fifth that day), part of which 'went down the wrong way'. A friend explained: 'There is a right way and a wrong way to eat a light bulb. Jim did it wrong.' Although he felt nothing immediately, he became ill the next day. Doctors were angry when they found that he was full of broken glass.

(from *The Guardian* and *The Daily Telegraph*)

Vocabulary: negatives

We use *un-*, *in-*, *dis-*, *non-* to make negatives.
Example:
*Jim Rose is an **unusual** man.*

a) Which word in each of these pairs is correct?
Use a dictionary to help you.

1 unhappy	inhappy
2 insense	nonsense
3 disagree	unagree
4 nonluckily	unluckily
5 unhonest	dishonest
6 nonstop	unstop
7 incorrect	discorrect
8 nonkind	unkind

b) Mark the stressed syllable in each correct
word. Example: *un'happy.*

Writing: improving a paragraph

Last night Fred was very unhappy. Fred decided
to go to a ✐ restaurant. Fred went alone. Fred
didn't want to go with the ✐ people who were
staying with Fred. Fred was very tired. Fred had
an argument with a ✐ waiter. Fred decided to go
home. Fred wanted to drive ✐ all the way. Fred
nearly fell asleep. Fred decided to stop. ✐ some
policemen saw Fred. The policemen asked Fred
what Fred was doing. Fred was angry. Fred
shouted at the policemen. The policemen
were angry. The policemen took Fred to the
police station.

Read the paragraph above.

a) Add one of the words in the box below in the
places marked ✐. You may have to change
a → an. Use each word once.

nonstop	unfriendly	inexpensive
unluckily	unpleasant	

b) Join the 16 sentences together to make 7–8
sentences. Use the words in the box below.

and	but	because	so	however	too

c) Do not repeat words again and again.
Use the words in the box below.

he	they	him	them

GRAMMAR

The passive

1 Read this extract from a newspaper article
and answer the questions.

Swedish youth stopped

The youth was stopped from working as an au pair
in Britain because he is male. He was
questioned at Heathrow airport when he arrived
and then

1 Are we more interested in the young man
or the people who stopped him?
2 Do we know the names of the people at
Heathrow airport who questioned him?
Are they important?

2 Look at these sentences and answer
the questions.

	SUBJECT	ACTIVE VERB	OBJECT
a)	*They*	*questioned*	*the youth.*

	SUBJECT	PASSIVE VERB
b)	*The youth*	*was questioned.*

In which sentence:

1 is the word *questioned* in the Past Simple?
2 is the word *questioned* a past participle?
3 did the subject do something to the object?
4 did someone (we don't know who) do
something to the subject?

3 Look at the box below and complete the
sentences.

> The passive is formed with *be* + the past participle.
>
> | *I* | **am / was** | | |
> |---|---|---|---|
> | *You / We / They* | **are / were** | **taken** | *to the police.* |
> | *He / She / It* | **is / was** | | |

ACTIVE
1 Someone stole my gloves yesterday.
PASSIVE
_____ yesterday.

ACTIVE
2 Someone hit Pat last night.
PASSIVE
_____ last night.

4   Find an example of the passive in the story on the right.

> With the passive we use *by* when we say who or what did something to the subject.

5   What is the passive form of these verbs?

1 give   it *is given* (PRESENT)
2 eat   they _____ (PRESENT)
3 meet   she _____ (PAST)
4 drink   it _____ (PAST)
5 build   it _____ (PAST)
6 make   they _____ (PRESENT)
7 sell   it _____ (PAST)

The postman was attacked by a dog while he was delivering letters. The animal bit his hand. The postman ran shouting for help while the dog was chasing him.

6   Complete these sentences with the correct form of the passive. The first two are done for you.

1 They were found in a forest.
  Where *were they found?* (question)
2 He was met at the airport.
  He *wasn't met at the airport.* (negative)
3 She's called Tania.
  What _____ ? (question)
4 We were given the right tickets.
  We _____ . (negative)

7   Complete these sentences with the correct form of the verb in brackets. Use the active or passive of the Past Simple.

1 The best-selling game *Monopoly (create)* _____ in the 1930s. In 1975 more Monopoly money *(print)* _____ in the USA than real money.
2 In the film *The Gold Rush* Charlie Chaplin *(eat)* _____ his boots. They *(make)* _____ of black sugar.
3 In 1985 part of Mexico City *(destroy)* _____ by an earthquake. Over 2,000 people *(kill)* _____ , but rescue workers *(find)* _____ over fifty newborn babies alive under a building.
4 In March 1944 Sergeant Alkemade's plane *(hit)* _____ by a gunshot and he *(jump)* _____ 5,485 metres without a parachute. He *(crash)* _____ into trees and *(find)* _____ safe and alive in the snow.

Using your grammar

1   Work in groups.

GROUP A: Look at page 128.
GROUP B: Look at the quiz on the right. Write full questions for numbers 4–6.

Answer all the questions. Then check your answers on page 126.

2   Ask the other group your questions. The group with the most correct answers wins.

1 When was Mount Everest first climbed? 1943, 1953 or 1963?
2 When is Hallowe'en celebrated? 31 September, 31 October or 31 November?
3 Where was the 1994 World Cup in soccer played? Italy, Spain or the USA?
4 Where / Martin Luther King / assassinated? Memphis, Dallas or New York?
5 Who / the play / *Hamlet* / written by? Homer, Shakespeare or Dickens?
6 In which country / champagne / produced? France, Germany or Italy?

VOCABULARY

News stories

Your stars
···················
Aries *21 March – 19 April*
This week you must organise your money. Cash which you have been waiting for may not come. Try to work off some of that extra energy with some exercise.
(b)

Killer shot dead
in gunfight (c)

Cooler in most places with heavy clouds some sunshine. Winds are strong from the
(d)

CHALET HOLIDAYS

(e) BEAUTIFUL SWITZERLAND
Family-run chalet
Personal service
Excellent food and accommodation
Skiing, sauna, open fires
Telephone 01799 501504

1   Look at the extracts from newspapers on the right. Which is:

1 a headline?   3 an advertisement?   5 a horoscope?
2 a cartoon?   4 a weather forecast?

2   Look at the headline and article below. The word 'meet' has the sound /iː/ . What other spelling does /miːt/ have?

> # No meet
> # for us
>
> Marie Abbott (56) and Tony Lom (46), two butchers from Worthing, missed the most important appointment of their lives when

3   Read the headlines below.

a)   What other spelling could the underlined word(s) have?

I LOVE YOU <u>TWO</u>   DEN'S <u>WAIT</u> PROBLEM   <u>GOOD BUY</u>!
A <u>PEACE</u> OF PAPER   <u>WRITE</u> AND WRONG

b)   Which headline is about:

  1 children whose homework is bad?
  2 a large person whose dinner didn't arrive on time?

4   Match the words in A and B to make expressions that often go together in news stories. Sometimes there is more than one possibility. Divide the expressions into two lists: 1 Good news; 2 Bad news.

A	B
car	record
bomb	champion
world	crash
tennis	block
road	explosion

Using your vocabulary

You are going to tell a news story about a traffic policeman.

a)   Use a dictionary to find the meanings of the words in the box.

throw away   baton   drivers   confused   lorry

b)   Work in groups.
GROUP A: Look at the picture on page 127.
GROUP B: Look at the picture on the right. What do you think is happening? What is going to happen? Now work with a partner from Group A. You start. Tell the story in your picture. Don't look at your partner's picture. Then listen while your partner tells his/her part of the story.

USE AND REVIEW

1   Read this newspaper article. Why were there more crimes in North Oxfordshire last year?

MY 1,800 THEFTS

A man who is a shoplifter and burglar has confessed to 1,800 crimes going back six years. The 25-year-old man lives in North Oxfordshire. He told his story after he got a two year prison sentence for burglary.

There were 24% more crimes in North Oxfordshire last year and 17% of them were his.

2   Look at the picture above. These are some of the things the police found. Talk about how much and how many things.
Examples:
They found a few traveller's cheques and a lot of cameras.

3   Sally and Kevin are talking about the criminal in the article above. Which are the correct words?

SALLY: I hear *someone / anyone / no one* was sent to prison for two years for burglary last week. *Anyone / No one* should go to prison for more than six months for a crime like that.

KEVIN: I don't agree. He confessed to 1,800 crimes. Have you heard of *someone / anyone / no one* who has committed so many crimes in North Oxfordshire?

SALLY: 1,800! That's *too much / too many* crimes for one person!

KEVIN: No, it's true. From some houses he didn't take *anything / nothing* important. Only silly things like bottles of Coke. *Everyone / Everything / Anyone* thinks he is crazy.

SALLY: That's terrible! I think he should go to prison for ten years. Two years is *very / too* short!

4   Work with a partner.

a) What do you think of the man's prison sentence?

b) What do you think of these punishments: 10 years in prison for murder, a £50 fine for dropping litter, 6 months in prison for stealing £5 and a £2,000 fine for robbing a bank? Use the words in the box.

too / very	long / short	little / much

Language reference

1 The passive

FORM

be (am / is / are) + past participle
The past participle of regular verbs is formed by adding *-ed* to the base form of the verb.
The past participles of common irregular verbs are on page 132.

Positive
She **is killed** *at the end of the film.* *French* **is spoken** *here.*
Negative
The window **isn't (is not) broken.** *This book* **wasn't (was not) written** *by a famous writer.* *Tea* **isn't (is not) grown** *in England.* *Cars* **aren't (are not) made** *in Madeira.*
Question
Is *the window* **broken?** *Why* **isn't** *tea* **grown** *in England?*

USE

We usually use the passive when we do not know, or are not interested in, who does something.
  Tea **is grown** in India.
When we want to use the passive and say who or what did the action we use *by*.
  Jill was met **by** *her brother.*

2 Active or passive?

In an active sentence we are usually more interested in **who** did the action.

Subject	Active verb	Object
Martin	*met*	*Jill.*

In a passive sentence we do not put the person who did the action at the beginning of the sentence.

Subject	Passive verb	
Jill	*was met*	**(by** *Martin).*

The object of an active sentence is the subject of a passive sentence.

•Celebration!•

USE YOUR ENGLISH

Special occasions

OCTOBER

Mon	Tue	Wed	Thu	Fri	Sat	Sun
		1	2	3	4	5
6	7	8	9	10	11	12
13	14	15	16	17	18	19
20	21	22	23	24	25	26
27	28	29	30	31		

NOVEMBER

Mon	Tue	Wed	Thu	Fri	Sat	Sun
	4	5	6	7	1	2
	11	12	13	14	8	9
18	19	20	21	15	16	
25	26	27	28	22	23	
			29	30		

FEBRUARY

Mon	Tue	Wed	Thu	Fri	Sat	Sun
						1
6	7	8				
13	14	15				
20	21	22				
27	28					

JANUARY

Mon	Tue	Wed	Thu	Fri	Sat	Sun
			1	2	3	4
	7	8	9	10	11	
14	15	16	17	18		
		23	24	25		
26						

DECEMBER

Mon	Tue	Wed	Thu	Fri	Sat	Sun
1	2	3	4	5	6	7
8	9	10	11	12	13	14
15	16	17	18	19	20	21
22	23	24	25	26	27	28
29	30	31				

1 The dates on the calendar are important in Britain. Do you know why? What happens on these days? Are any of them important in your country?

2 [17.1] Listen to these conversations.

a) Match the conversations with the dates on the calendar.
b) Find dates which match the pictures on the right.

3 What do we say on some important days? Match the words in A with those in B. For *Happy* there is more than one possibility.

A	B
Merry	New Year!
Happy	a good time!
Have	Christmas!
	birthday!

4 Work with a partner. Read these conversations.

1 A: I'm taking my driving test later today.
  B: Good luck!
2 A: It's my eighteenth birthday today.
  B: Congratulations!

a) In what other situations do we say 'Good luck!' and 'Congratulations!'?
b) Write short conversations for some of the situations.
c) Practise the conversations with your partner.

5 Work with a partner. Which dates do you think are important in your country? Tell him/her why.

SKILLS

Reading

1   Look at the pictures. What do you think Chinese New Year is like?

2   Read the article on the right about Chinese New Year and match the paragraphs with these questions. Example: 1 = C

1 How was the festival traditionally celebrated?
2 Why did the Chinese Government say there must be no more fireworks?
3 How long do the celebrations last?
4 How have the Chinese New Year celebrations changed?
5 What animal did 1994 have the name of?

3   Read the article again.

a) Make some notes about these questions.

   1 What do young people in China think? Example:
     They don't believe in superstitions.
   2 What happened when families went to other
     people's houses?
   3 What religious traditions are there at New Year?

b) Work with a partner. Compare your notes.

Vocabulary

1   What do these words mean? Choose a) or b). Can you guess from the article? Use a dictionary to help you, if necessary.

1 lanterns *n* (paragraph C)	a) bags	b) lights
2 lasted *v* (paragraph D)	a) continued	b) finished
3 banned *v* (paragraph E)	a) began	b) stopped

2   Find a word or expression that means:

1 shut *v* (paragraph A)
2 became adults *v* (paragraph D)
3 hurt *v* (paragraph E)
4 not dangerous *adj* (paragraph E)

A   **T**he New Year's Festival in China can be in January or February. Although it is only a four-day holiday, China's offices often close down for nearly a month.

B   Every year has the name of one of the twelve animals of the Chinese zodiac, such as a cow, a rabbit or a monkey. 1994 was the year of the dog. People who are born in the year of the dog are believed to be quiet, faithful and friendly. If you were born in a dog year, then, as soon as the New Year begins, you should wear a red belt around your waist for good luck. However, young people in China do not believe in the superstition. 'I wore a belt when it was my year,' says 32-year-old driver Xiao Hung, 'and I had a lot of bad luck. I took it off.'

C   Mai-Tai remembers the New Year celebrations when she was a girl in the 1950s. In the evenings parents and children used to go on visits to the houses of their relatives and friends. They held lanterns to give them light in the dark streets. All around them, they could hear fireworks in the cold air. The door of each house had long pieces of red paper on it. Everywhere they went food was waiting for them, and they ate until they couldn't move. Relatives used to give the children money.

D   During the Cultural Revolution, which lasted from 1966 to 1976, religious traditions were stopped in China. But in the 1980s people once again began to kneel before the names of their ancestors at New Year. However, as many young people grew up during the Revolution, they aren't interested in the old traditions. They have started to celebrate some of the Western festivals like Christmas.

E   One part of the New Year which worried the Chinese Government was the tradition of fireworks, which got bigger and louder. In the countryside, fireworks were more like small bombs and hundreds of people were injured and killed. But in 1994 the Government banned fireworks to make the New Year safe for everyone.

Writing: paragraphs

1　Read this paragraph.
Put sentences 1–4 in the
correct order.

*Christmas is the most important
public holiday in Britain.*
1 On Christmas Day people give
  presents to each other and eat
  a large dinner.
2 Before Christmas, carols
  are sung and people send
  Christmas cards to their
  friends and relatives.
3 The day after Christmas Day is
  called Boxing Day and is also
  a public holiday.
4 Most people spend the
  holiday with their families.
*Although Christmas was
originally a Christian festival,
many people today feel that it is
not religious any more.*

2　Answer these questions
and make notes about a special
festival in your country.

1 How do people celebrate
  the festival?
2 What do people feel about
  the festival?

3　Write a paragraph using
your notes.
Begin your paragraph: *In my
country …*
Middle sentences: Describe the
festival.
Last sentence: What do people
feel about the festival?

4　Ask yourself these
questions about your paragraph.

1 Is the paragraph clear and
  easy to understand?
2 Are the verb forms correct?
3 Are the linking expressions
  correct?
4 Are the spelling and
  punctuation correct?

GRAMMAR

Present Perfect Continuous: the unfinished past

1　Jon is a writer.

a) [🔲 17.2]　Read and listen to this conversation.
Then answer the questions.

ROSA: It's your birthday. You're not working, are you?
JON:　I'm afraid so. I want to finish this novel.
ROSA: How long have you been writing it?
JON:　Oh, for ages – since Christmas.

1 When did Jon start the novel?
2 Is he still writing it?

b) Look at the box and the pictures below. Complete the
sentences with the Present Perfect Continuous. Use the verb in
brackets.

> I've
> He's | **been writing** *a novel for three months.*
>
> The Present Perfect Continuous is formed with *has/have been + -ing*
> form of the verb.

1 Jon _____ on a novel since Christmas. *(work)*
2 She _____ computer games all morning. *(play)*
3 'I _____ Spanish since February.' *(learn)*

2 [▭ 17.3] Jon and Rosa meet again in November. Read and listen to their conversation. Then answer the questions.

ROSA: Have you finished your novel yet?

JON: Yes. I finished it three weeks ago. I've written two short stories since then.

ROSA: Wow! What are you doing at the moment?

JON: I'm writing a play for television. I've been working on it for the last week.

ROSA: Amazing!

1 What has Jon written since he finished his novel?
2 Are the stories finished?
3 When did he start his play for television?
4 Is he still writing it?
5 Which verb forms are often used to talk about an action which started in the past and continues to the present? (See the *Language reference* on page 107 for verbs that do not usually take the *-ing* form.)

3 Read these sentences.

a) Which is the correct verb?

1 *Have you read / Have you been reading* that newspaper yet? Can I have it?
2 How long *have you been cleaning / have you cleaned* that car? *Haven't you finished / Haven't you been finishing* it yet?
3 How long *have you known / have you been knowing* Rosa?
4 He *is living / has been living* in Manchester since 1990.
5 She *has liked / has been liking* you since she saw you at that party.
6 I'm sorry I'm late. How long *are you waiting / have you been waiting*?
7 *I've played / I've been playing* tennis twice this week.
8 It's *been raining / is raining* here all morning. It started at eight.

b) [▭ 17.4] Listen and check your answers.

4 [▭ 17.5] Listen to these conversations. How are these words pronounced: *has, have, been*?

1 A: How long has she been cleaning the car?
  B: For ages.
2 A: How long have you been living in Manchester?
  B: Since 1990.
3 A: Are you angry?
  B: Yes. I've been waiting for two hours.
4 A: How long has it been raining?
  B: All morning.

For and *since*

We use *since* to refer to a point in time (*1983, last week, our last holiday*) and *for* to refer to a period of time (*five years, four hours, a long time, ages*).

a) Do these expressions go with *for* or *since*?

six weeks	March
a year	yesterday
we met	my birthday
14 June	a few days
the end of the lesson	
6.45	three minutes

b) Make sentences with the Present Perfect Simple or Continuous and *for* or *since*. Example:
I / be a policeman / I left school
I've been a policeman since I left school.

1 he / watch television / three hours
2 she / not see him / a long time
3 he / talk on the phone / lunch time
4 they / play football / 3 o'clock
5 we / be married / 10 years

Using your grammar

On a piece of paper write ten things about yourself. Use the Present Simple or the Present Continuous. Write about:
- what you are wearing now.
- a habit.
- what your family and friends do.
- what you do in your free time.
- a place you often go to.

Work in groups. Mix up the papers. Take a piece of paper and guess who wrote it. Ask the person questions beginning *How long ...?* (Example: *How long have you had that jumper?*)

VOCABULARY

Having a party

1   Replace the underlined words with the correct form of the words from the box.

> soft   celebrate   enjoy yourself

2   Which is the correct word?

1 A: Do you like parties?
   B: No, I find them *boring / bored / exciting*.
2 A: Hey, look at the band! Aren't they great?
   B: Yes, I always prefer *recorded / live* music.
3 A: Is John *drunk / sober*?
   B: Yes, I'm afraid he is. He can't stand up!

1   A: Are you <u>having a good time</u>?   B: Yes, it's a great party.

2   A: What are we <u>having a party for</u>?   B: Cindy's twenty-first birthday.

3   A: What about a glass of wine?   B: Haven't you got any <u>non-alcoholic</u> drinks?

3   People often make mistakes with the words in italics.

a)   Which is the correct word?

1 London has many *visitors / guests* every year.
2 My sister is a very good *cooker / cook*.
3 We study at a language school for *strangers / foreign students*.
4 We took a guided *tour / trip* round the museum.
5 Can you *learn / teach* me how to play the guitar?
6 I *lent / borrowed* you £50. Give it back.
7 Have you *passed / past* your exams?

b)   Make sentences with three of the other words. Example:
We had fifty guests at our party last night.

Using your vocabulary

1   What makes a good party? Which of these ideas do you agree with? Add some ideas of your own.

- The best parties are always at the weekend and go on all night.
- There should be the same number of men and women.
- The music should be loud.
- There should be a lot of good food and drink.
- There should be a lot of games.
- The people should all know each other.
- There should be decorations.

2   Work in groups. You are going to have a party. Talk about the questions below. Then tell the class about your party.

1 What is the party for? (your sister's birthday? your class?)
2 Where? (at the school? at a restaurant?)
3 When? (in the middle of the day?)
4 Who should come? (a few friends? other students? everyone?)
5 What kind of food do you want?
6 What kind of music do you want?

USE AND REVIEW

1   Work with a partner.

a) STUDENT A
Look at page 127.

STUDENT B
What are the past participles of these verbs:
hear, sell, wear, break, understand, put, think,
say, speak?

b) Ask your partner about the past participles
of your verbs. Write down his/her answers.
Don't say if the answer is correct or not.
Example:
B: *What is the past participle of hear?*
A: *Heard.*

c) Your partner is going to ask you about some
past participles.

d) Check your answers on page 129. Who got
the most correct answers?

2   These are some pieces of 'good news'.
Write the 'bad news'. Use the words in brackets
to help you. Use the passive. Example:
The art gallery bought the painting for $1 million.
(steal / last night)
The painting was stolen last night.

1 The singer is giving a concert in Rome.
   (tickets / sell out)
2 I saw an expensive glass bowl in the shop.
   (break / child)
3 There was a bottle of wine in the cupboard.
   (drink / last week)
4 John looked well yesterday morning.
   (take to hospital / yesterday evening)
5 The President was very popular. *(assassinate
   in 1994 / someone from another country)*

3   Make sentences from these headlines. Are
they good or bad news?

(a) **Airport closed
by bad weather**

(b) **More CDs
sold last year**

**FILM STAR'S
NEW BABY**

(d) **Ice-skater
breaks leg**

(e) **MISSING
SCULPTURE
FOUND**

(f) **Train crash
in Sweden**

Language reference

1 Present Perfect Continuous

FORM

Have/has + *been* + base form of verb + *-ing*

Positive
*I've **been playing*** all day.
Negative
*She **hasn't been playing*** all day.
Question
*How long **have** they **been playing?***
Have** you **been playing for a long time?

USE

We use the Present Perfect Continuous to talk about things
that started in the past and are still going on now.
   *I've **been living** here since 1992.* (I started living here
   in 1992 and I am still living here.)

← ⎯⎯⎯ x I've **been living** here ⎯⎯⎯ →

PAST   since   for a long   NOW
              1992   time

Note that we do NOT say: ~~I'm living here since 1992~~.

2 *For* or *since*?

For (**for** a long time) and *since* (**since** 1992) say how long
something has been happening.
   How long have you been learning French?
   I've been learning French | **for** six months.
                                | **since** 1994.
For is used with a period of time. (**for** two years, six
months, a long time)
Since is used with a point in time. (**since** 1992, July, 10.30,
4th June)

3 Present Perfect Simple or Present Perfect Continuous?

We can also use the Present Perfect Simple to talk about
events that started in the past and are still going on now.
   *I've **lived** here since 1992.*
There is often little difference between the Present Perfect
Continuous and the Present Perfect Simple. However we
usually use the Present Perfect Continuous when we are
thinking of the action.
   *I've **been working** here since 1982.*
Verbs that express a state, not an action, do **not** usually
take an *-ing* form:
like, know, love, be, have.
   *I've **liked** you since I saw you at the disco.*
Note that we do NOT say: ~~I've been liking you...~~

•Love your neighbour•

USE YOUR ENGLISH

Being polite

1   Look at the pictures.

a) What do you think the people are saying?
b) [⊟ 18.1]   Listen to these conversations. Match the conversations with the pictures.
c) Complete these sentences.

1 Oh, _____ give me a hand with these, please?
2 Oh, _____ get me some stamps, please?
3 _____ but have you got any change?
4 Tom. Excuse me, _____ give me a push?
5 _____ looking after Oscar for a few days?

d) Which expression/s do we use when:

1 we don't know the other person very well?
2 we think the request is difficult for the other person?

e) Someone asks you to do something. What do you say when:

1 you agree to the request?
2 you don't agree to the request?

2   Work in groups. Ask each other to do things politely. Use the nouns and verbs in the boxes or use your own words. If you do not agree to the request, you must give a good reason.

NOUNS	VERBS
window pencil board £5 door seat time	lend open/close draw pick up take clean tell move write

3   Work with a partner. Write conversations for some of these situations.

1 You want a taxi driver to drive you from London to Edinburgh.
2 You ordered a salad but the waiter has brought you a steak.
3 You are locked out of your flat. You want a neighbour to help you get in.
4 You are in front of the White House in Washington and you want a stranger to take a photograph of you.
5 It's three o'clock in the morning. You have a plane to catch at seven and must get some sleep. Ask your friend to wake you at five.

SKILLS

Listening and speaking

1 What are the advantages and disadvantages of living in this kind of house? The two men are neighbours. They are having an argument. What do you think the problem is?

a) What do you think? Complete these sentences.

1 Having neighbours is good because _____.
2 Having neighbours is bad because _____.
3 I'd love to have neighbours who _____.
4 I'd hate to have neighbours who _____.

b) Work with a partner. Compare your answers and tell each other about your neighbours.

2 Work in two groups.

GROUP A
[📼 18.2] Listen to Henry Skitt talking about his neighbour, Tim Dodd, and his friends. Answer these questions.

1 What does Henry think of his neighbours' music?
2 What did the police do about it?
3 Why hasn't Henry been to work?
4 What do the young people do in Henry's garden?
5 If Tim told Henry he was going to have a party, what would Henry do?

GROUP B
[📼 18.3] Listen to Tim Dodd talking about Mr Skitt. Answer these questions.

1 What didn't Tim know about Henry?
2 When does Tim play loud music? Why?
3 When was the last time Tim had a party?
4 What noise does Tim hear from his neighbour?
5 Why does Tim play his drums in the cellar?

3 Work with a partner from the other group. Ask for the answers to their questions.

4 Talk to your partner about these questions.

1 Is Henry Skitt right to complain? Give your reasons.
2 What advice would you give Henry and Tim?
3 Should it be against the law to make too much noise? Give your reasons.
4 In your country, can you ask the police to come if your neighbours make too much noise?
5 Which of these can/can't you do where you live?

- have a pet
- hang washing outside
- have an untidy garden
- leave rubbish outside
- beep your car horn at night

6 Are there any other rules where you live?

Vocabulary: phrasal verbs

Here are some phrasal verbs which Henry and Tim used.

- *I have to **lie down**.*
- *I've been **off** work.*
- *They can always **come round**.*
- *We're not going to **get into** a fight.*
- *I play music to **wake** myself **up**.*

Use them to complete the sentences.

1 Will you _____ _____ to my house and see me later?
2 I feel tired. I'm going to _____ _____ on the bed for a few minutes. Can you _____ me _____ at six?
3 I don't want to _____ _____ an argument about who's right and who's wrong.
4 Julia isn't well. She is going to _____ _____ school tomorrow.

Writing: phrasal verbs

Phrasal verbs are usually informal. Rewrite these notes. Replace the underlined words with one of the phrasal verbs in brackets. Use the correct form of the verb.

1 Take the motorway and <u>leave</u> at the first exit. Ring the bell when you <u>arrive</u> at the house.
(turn up, turn off)

2 I'm going to <u>stop coming</u> here if you don't repair the lift. It <u>stopped working</u> again this morning.
(give up, break down)

3 Sorry I was late home last night, darling. I had to <u>go somewhere with</u> an important customer. I hope you didn't <u>keep awake</u> waiting for me.
(stay up, take out)

GRAMMAR

Sentence patterns (1): verb + person

1 Read this extract from a famous children's story.

'I'm going shopping in the village,' George's mother said to George on Saturday morning. 'So be a good boy ... And don't forget to give Grandma her medicine at eleven o'clock.' Then out she went, closing the back door behind her.

	SUBJECT	VERB	OBJECT/ PERSON	TO + BASE FORM OF VERB
'Be a good boy,' George's mother said.	She	**told**	George	to be a good boy.
'Don't forget to give Grandma her medicine,' George's mother said.	She	**asked**	him	**not** to forget to give Grandma her medicine.

2 Read the next part of the story and complete the sentences.

'Now you heard what your mother said, George. Don't forget my medicine.'
'No, Grandma,' George said.
'And try to behave well while she is away.'
'Yes, Grandma,' George said.

1 Grandma _____ George not to _____.
2 Grandma _____ George to _____ well.

3 Read the next part of the story.

'You can make me a nice cup of tea for a start,'
Grandma said to George.
'Yes, Grandma,' George said.
George really disliked Grandma.
'How much sugar in your tea today, Grandma?' he asked her.
'One spoon,' she said. 'And no milk ...'
George went into the kitchen and made Grandma a cup of tea
with a teabag. He put one spoon of sugar in it and no milk.
He stirred the tea well and carried the cup into the living room.
Grandma sipped the tea. 'It's not sweet enough,' she said.
'Put more sugar in.'

(from *George's Marvellous Medicine* by Roald Dahl)

Make sentences with the words below. Example:
She / make / nice cup of tea.
She told/asked George to make her a nice cup of tea.

1 She / put in / one spoon   2 She / not / put any milk in.
  of sugar.   3 She / put more sugar in.

Sentence patterns (2): reported sentences

Say or *tell*?

'I'm only a little boy, Grandma,' George said.		
	OBJECT / PERSON	
George **said**		(that) he **was** only a little boy.
George **told**	Grandma / her	

a) Complete these sentences with *said* or *told*.

1 Sarah _____ me it was her birthday.
2 He _____ he didn't like tennis.
3 She _____ Mike they never went out.
4 Nikki _____ she knew the way.
5 Carlos _____ her not to shout.

b) Write reported sentences with *say* or *tell*. Example:
  'I'm going out.'   *John said he was going out.*

1 'We want to see the film.'   Sally and Peter _____.
2 'I'm watching television later.' Tony _____.
3 'We like Disneyland.'   Emma _____ her _____.
4 'I'm very happy.'   Mary _____.
5 'Greg is hungry.'   Tina _____ Sonia that _____.

Using your grammar

Work in groups of three.

STUDENT A
Look at page 127.

STUDENT B
You are from the same family
as Student A. Choose how
you are related. Are you
husband and wife, brother
and sister, parent and child?
You have had an argument.
You are angry with Student A
because he/she:
• gives orders
• gets up early and makes
  a noise.
• never wants to go out.

Make a list of other things
you are angry about (money,
parties, TV, clothes, car etc).
Your aren't speaking to
Student A but Student C is a
go-between. Ask him/her to
help you.

STUDENT C
Student A and Student B
aren't speaking to each other.
You are a go-between. Help
Students A and B with their
lists. Begin with Student B.
Tell Student B about Student
A and Student A about
Student B. Examples:
*He says you are lazy. She
told me you never help in
the house. She asked me to
tell you ...*
Try to get Students A and B
to be friends again.

VOCABULARY

Doing things in the house

Look at the pictures on the right.

a) Match them with the verbs in the box.

| iron | decorate | dust | hoover | wash up | tidy up |

b) Make sentences about the pictures using the words in the box.
Example:
He's doing the ironing.

c) What other jobs are there to do in the house?

Do or *make*?

> DO – work, general action
> They **did** the ironing.   He **did** the housework.   She **did** her homework.
>
> MAKE – create something, a particular action
> He **made** a pizza.   He **made** a mistake.   They **made** a noise.
>
> Note: **make** the bed = tidy the sheets and blankets

Complete these sentences with the correct form of *do* or *make*.
Use a dictionary to help you.

1 A: Hurry up. You must _____ the cleaning.
  B: No, I hate _____ housework.
2 A: Sorry, dear. I've _____ a mistake. I _____ you a cup
     of tea but I put salt in it instead of sugar!
  B: You idiot! And you've _____ a mess in the kitchen.
     Can't you _____ anything right?
  A: Shall I go and _____ the washing?
  B: No. I'll _____ that. You go and _____ the bed.
3 A: Why do your children always _____ such a noise?
     Why don't you keep them quiet?
  B: Sorry, but I _____ my best.

Using your vocabulary

Look at the pictures on the right.

a) In your country which jobs do men do? Which jobs do women
do? Which jobs do *you* do? Make three lists.
b) Who does the jobs which you don't do?
c) Work with a partner. Compare your lists.

USE AND REVIEW

1   Talk to other students in the class.
Find someone who:

1 can tell you the difference between a *stranger*
  and a *foreigner*.
2 knows another word for a *non-alcoholic* drink.
3 can explain the difference between a *cooker*
  and a *cook*.
4 knows what *live* music is.
5 can give you one sentence with *lend* and
  one sentence with *borrow*.

2   Work in two groups.

GROUP A: You are John Smith. You want a job as
        the editor of a newspaper in the USA.
GROUP B: You are Sophie Evans. You want a job
        as an airline pilot in Australia.

a) Fill in this application form for your person.

APPLICATION FORM FOR THE JOB OF

_____

NAME

AGE   DATE OF BIRTH

EXPERIENCE   *I have worked ...*

              I have lived ...

              I have been studying ...

PRESENT OCCUPATION   *I am working ...*

INTERESTS   *I like ...*

---

b) Work with a partner from the other group.
    Read your partner's application form and then
    interview him/her for the job. Ask questions
    with *what / when / how long have you ...?*

Language reference

1 Subject + verb + person + *to* + base form of the verb

Subject	Verb	Object person	*To* + Base form
'Go!' I/ You/ We/ They He/ She/ It	asked told	her/ him/ it	to go.
'Don't go!' I/ You/ We/ They He/ She/ It	asked told	us/me/you/them	**not** to go.

2 *Say* or *tell*?

We *say* **something**.
   He says (that) **it is late**.
We *tell* **a person** something.
   He told **us** *(that) he was not very well.*

3 Reported sentences

We use this form when we report what a person said.
Exact words:
   'I'm going out.'
Reported words:
   He says (that) he is going out.
   He said (that) he was going out.
   He said to me (that) he was going out.
   He tells me (that) he's going out.
   He told me (that) he was going out.
When we use *said* or *told* (past tense) the reported
statement (*'I'm going out'*) is often in the past.
   He **said**/**told** *me he* **was going** *out.*
It is not necessary to use *that*.

•Team spirit•

USE YOUR ENGLISH

Talking about different cultures

1 Look at the pictures. Ayu has just arrived in Britain from Indonesia.

a) What is Zoë saying? Can you guess? She is telling Ayu what to do:

   A to order drinks in a pub.
   B if she is invited to someone's house for dinner.
   C to attract the waiter's attention in a restaurant.
   D when she greets someone for the first time.
   E if she stays with a family.

b) [🖵 19.1] Listen to extracts from Zoë and Ayu's conversation. Match each extract with one of the pictures.

c) Listen again. What advice does Zoë give?
Example:
Always order at the bar.

d) What are the differences between Britain and your country?

2 In your country are there any laws about:

- dropping litter?
- riding bicycles?
- when shops can and can't open?
- crossing the road?

3 In your country are there any rules or customs about:

- giving your seat to old people on a bus?
- how people should dress? (for example, at work)
- tipping? (for example, in a taxi)
- people touching each other? (for example, in the street)
- greeting each other?
- what you do when you watch a sport? (for example, do you clap? do you boo? do you shout?)
- giving and receiving presents?

4 Work with a partner. A British tourist is coming to your country. Make a list of DOs and DON'Ts like the example on the right.

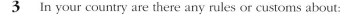

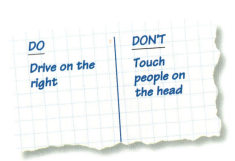

DO	DON'T
Drive on the right	Touch people on the head

SKILLS

Reading

1   Look at the picture and answer these questions.

1 How many *teams* are there?
2 What is the *stadium*?
3 Who is the *referee*?
4 Where are the *supporters*?
5 Which player has *scored* a *goal*?
6 Manchester United are playing in Manchester.
  Is it a *home match* or an *away match*?
7 At the end of the match the score was
  Manchester United 3, Chelsea 1. Who *won*?
8 Did Chelsea *beat* Manchester?

2   Read the article. Which
paragraphs tell us the answers to
these questions? Example: 1=*B*

1 How did Sister Paola first
  become interested in football?
2 How did she first become a
  TV star?
3 What do the Lazio players
  think of her?
4 What was the result of the
  Lazio-Milan game?

Team spirit

3   Answer these questions.

1 What is the 'big day'?
  (paragraph A)
2 Why is the referee a 'cheat'?
  (paragraph A)
3 When does Sister Paola
  punch the air?
4 How long has she liked
  football?
5 What does she do with the
  Lazio players?

4   These are some answers.
What are the questions?
Example: Lazio.
*Which team does Sister Paola
support?*

1 Twenty years ago.
2 No, AC Milan beat Lazio.
3 She goes back to her teaching.

A   he crowds are in Rome's Olympic Stadium for the big day. Their team, Lazio, are playing AC Milan. Millions of people are sitting in front of their TV sets. 'The referee is a cheat,' cries a well-known voice. 'That's why he didn't allow our team's great goal – but then, he comes from Milan!' This is Sister Paola, a 46-year-old nun. She is mad about Lazio. When they score, she punches the air. When they miss an easy goal, she covers her face.

B   She became a Lazio supporter twenty years ago when some children asked her to teach them about the game. She says: 'I thought I'd better go and watch Lazio. Then I became very keen on football.' So every Sunday when Lazio play at home – after attending Mass – Sister Paola walks down from the convent to the stadium, talking to the fans.

C   Then, recently, she learnt that the father of one of her pupils was a television sports reporter. She asked to go into the studio to see Lazio's away games. There a TV director thought he saw a possible star. The only question was, what would a nun, without make-up, and wearing simple clothes, be like on camera, with a microphone in her hand?

D   She was very good. People love to listen to her with her passion and love of football. And she is just as popular with the Lazio players. 'I talk about their problems and say prayers with them,' she says.

E   But today against the champions her prayers are not enough. AC Milan have beaten Lazio 1-0. The colour in her pale face disappears and her voice gets quieter. 'I don't know what to say,' she tells her fans. 'This is a terrible moment for us all.'

F   Then she returns to her work of the week, her prayers and her teaching, her prison visiting and her work with the poor.

(from *The Mail on Sunday*)

Vocabulary

Find a word or phrase in the article about Sister Paola that means:

1 large numbers of people (paragraph A)
2 hits with the hand closed (paragraph A)
3 puts her hands in front of it (paragraph A)
4 strong feelings (paragraph D)
5 almost white (paragraph E)

Writing

1　Read this sentence and answer the questions.
'The referee is a cheat,' cries a well-known voice.

1 What are Sister Paola's words?
2 Which punctuation marks show her words?
3 Where is the comma?

2　Punctuate these sentences:

1 Im going out she said
2 What are you thinking he asked her
3 I wont do it I told him

3　Rewrite this story. Use speech marks and commas where necessary.

She told me about her husband. He's a Chelsea supporter. Really? I said. How could you live with him? She saw the look on my face. Why don't you tell him to support Manchester United or you'll divorce him?
She laughed. You're crazy, you know. Really crazy she said.

GRAMMAR

Verb patterns (1): the future

If, when, as soon as, unless

1　Tim is 14. His Swiss uncle has invited him to go on holiday in Switzerland. He has booked a hotel room for Tim. Tim is saying goodbye to his parents.

a) [🔊 19.2]　Listen and complete the sentences.

1 What are you going to do when you _____ there?
2 I'll call you as soon as I _____.
3 What will you do if he _____ not there when you _____?
4 He won't come and pick you up unless you _____.

b)　What verb form do we use after *if, when, as soon as* and *unless* to talk about the future?

c)　Read these sentences.
When you see him, give him our love.
If you see him, give him our love.

1 In which sentence will Tim definitely see his uncle?
2 In which sentence is it possible he won't see him?

d)　Which is the correct word?

1 *When / If* it's fine tomorrow, we'll go for a swim. I hope it is.
2 *When / If* you get back from your trip, I'll cook you a nice meal. See you next week.

e)　*Unless* usually means 'if not'. Complete these sentences with *if* or *unless*. Examples:
Unless you hurry, you'll miss the plane.
If you don't hurry, you'll miss the plane.

1 _____ he phones, tell him I'm out.
2 _____ you are careful, you'll have an accident.

2　*As soon as* is like *when*. It means *at the moment that*. Complete these sentences. Use the correct form of the word in brackets. Example:
As soon as I see him, I *(tell)* _____ him.
As soon as I see him, I'll tell him.

1 Don't forget to clean your teeth when you *(get up)* _____.
2 You won't pass your exams unless you *(study)* _____.
3 If you know the answer, please *(not tell)* _____ me.
4 I'll buy some coffee as soon as the shop *(open)* _____.
5 Unless we hurry, we *(be)* _____ late.
6 When I see her, I *(invite)* _____ her.
7 There are a lot of trains. Don't worry if you *(miss)* _____ it.
8 As soon as it stops snowing, we *(go)* _____ out.

Verb patterns (2)

Verb + 2 objects

Tim's mother says, '*Give it to him as soon as you see him.*'

When *give* has two objects we can make the sentence in two ways.

Give	THING/OBJECT the **present** (noun) *it* (pronoun)	→ •	PERSON/OBJECT *to your* **uncle** (noun). *to* **him** (pronoun).
Give	PERSON/OBJECT *your* **uncle** (noun) **him** (pronoun)	←	THING/OBJECT the **present** (noun).

We don't usually say *Give your uncle* **it** or *Give him* **it**.

1   John is talking to Simon. Read these sentences and answer the questions.

a) *Give the camera to your brother.*

b) *Give it to your brother.*

c) *Give your brother the camera.*

1 What does John tell Simon to give?
2 Who must Simon give it to?
3 In each sentence above underline the answer to 1.
4 In each sentence circle the answer to 2.
5 What preposition comes after the thing and before the person?

2   Look at the *Language reference* on page 119.

a) Which other verbs follow the same patterns as *give?*
b) Write sentences with these words. Put them in the correct order. Add any other necessary words. Begin: *Please ...*

1 him / the message / give
2 later / it / give / her
3 the book / him / take
4 the children / read / a story
5 the way / me / show
6 the money / me / lend

3   What do you think the people below are saying?

Using your grammar

Work with a partner. Write some instructions for a secret agent's next job.

a) Think about the answers to these questions.

- What is the mission? (to steal a bomb? to stop someone killing the president?)
- Who is the agent going to meet? (another agent? the president's wife?)

b) Write instructions using *when, if, as soon as, unless.* Examples:
When you get there, go to the ... (hotel, palace)
If you see him, give him the ... (message, photos)
Unless you ... (say the password, carry a gun)

a

pass

b   c

bring   send

d

show

VOCABULARY

Sports

1   Look at the pictures and say what the sport is.

a) Find a word from the box for each picture.

costume	ring	club	pool	course	pitch
gloves	track	shorts	court	ball	racket

b) What other words from the box go with each picture?
Example: 1 = *court*

2   Do we use *go* or *play* with these sports? Use a dictionary to help you.

jogging	basketball	skiing	baseball
windsurfing	squash	ice-skating	football

3   What is happening in the pictures on the right?

a) Match the pictures with these sentences.

  1 The horse *kicked* me.
  2 Jane *hit* him on the head with a book.
  3 He *ran* to catch the bus.
  4 She *threw* her coat on the floor.
  5 Tom *bounced* the baby on his knee.
  6 He *punched* the man on the nose.

b) Find a sport in Exercises 1 and 2 above for each of the verbs in italics in Exercise 3a). Example: kick = *football*

Using your vocabulary

1   What exercise do you take? How often do you do it? Examples:
I walk home every evening. I do exercises every morning. I go swimming once a week. I do the housework on Saturdays.

2   Find the student in the class who is most similar to you.

USE AND REVIEW

1   Write down five true and five false sentences about yourself. Examples:
I live on a boat. My father works in a bank.

a) Work with a partner. Choose someone you don't know very well. Guess if your partner's sentences are true.

b) Report back to the class. Example:
Thomas told me he lived on a boat but it's not true.

2   Look at this picture above for one minute and close your books.

a) What can you remember? Write down as many sentences as you can. Example:
A woman is making the bed upstairs.

b) Work with a partner. Compare your sentences.

Language reference

1 Verb patterns (1): the future with *if, when, as soon as, unless*

When we use the conjunctions *if, when, as soon as* and *unless* to talk about the future, we use a present verb form (often the Present Simple).

FORM

	Present		
If **When** **As soon as**	*it's*		*sunny, I'll go out.*
Unless	*it's*		*sunny, I won't go out.*

USE

a) *when*
    When means it's sure to happen.
    I'm going to Oxford. **When** *I'm there, I'll see my brother.*

b) *if*
    If means it will possibly happen.
    Perhaps I'll go to Oxford. **If** *I go, I'll see my brother.*

c) *unless*
    Unless means *if not.*
    I can't hear you **unless** *you shout.*
    (*I can't hear you* **if** *you do**n't** shout.*)

d) *as soon as*
    As soon as means *when /at the moment that.*
    I'll leave **as soon as** *I can.*

2 Verb patterns (2): Verb + 2 objects

Some verbs have two objects.

a) Pattern 1

	Verb	Person (Indirect object)	Thing (Direct object)
I	*gave*	*my friend* *him*	*a car.*

b) Pattern 2

	Verb	Thing (Direct object)	Person (*to* + Indirect object)
I	*gave*	*a car* *it*	*to my friend.* *to him.*

Other verbs which follow the same patterns: *read, show, pass, bring, send, lend, pay, sell, take.*
Note that we cannot say: ~~*I gave my friend it.*~~

•Going away•

USE YOUR ENGLISH

Booking in

1   Anna booked into a hotel this afternoon.

a) What did she do? Put the pictures in the correct order and then make sentences.

b) Can you complete her conversation with the receptionist?

unpack / suitcase

RECEPTIONIST:	Good afternoon. Can I _____ ?
ANNA:	Yes, I've _____ a room for two nights.
RECEPTIONIST:	_____ ?
ANNA:	Anna Escobar.
RECEPTIONIST:	Single or _____ ?
ANNA:	Single.
RECEPTIONIST:	Do you want a room with a _____ or a shower ?
ANNA:	A shower, please.
RECEPTIONIST:	Just _____ this form, please.
ANNA:	Certainly. How much _____ a night?
RECEPTIONIST:	£68 with breakfast. How _____ ?
ANNA:	With American Express. Is that OK?
RECEPTIONIST:	Fine. How much _____ ?
ANNA:	Just these two suitcases.
RECEPTIONIST:	_____ is 220. Breakfast _____ 7.00 to 9.30. _____ an evening meal?
ANNA:	No, thanks. _____ a traveller's cheque later?
RECEPTIONIST:	Of course, here's your key. Enjoy your stay.

c) [🔲 20.1]   Listen and check your answers.

2   Work with a partner.

> **STUDENT A**
> Look at page 128.

> **STUDENT B**
> You are the receptionist at the Swan Hotel. Use the information on the right to answer Student A's questions.

hotel bus / from airport

porter / tip

check in / reception

Swan Hotel

Large house 2 miles from city centre in quiet residential area.
Friendly family atmosphere.
Some bedrooms with private bathroom or shower.
En-suite toilets in many rooms.
Central heating six months of the year.
Comfortable restaurant overlooking the garden.
Small cocktail bar.
Street parking nearby.
TV room.
No pets or children.
Price per person per night: £75.

SKILLS

Reading and speaking

1   These people had bad holiday experiences. What do you think happened to them?

2   Work in three groups.

GROUP A

a) Read Maureen's postcard. Which picture does it describe?

b) Complete these sentences.

1 On Maureen's earlier holiday in Florida there were _____.
2 When she went to Australia _____.
3 She thought this holiday was going to be different because she was _____.
4 Unfortunately, at the airport she took _____.

GROUP B

a) Read Leslie's postcard. Which picture does it describe?

b) Complete these sentences.

1 Leslie wanted to catch _____.
2 He took his wife and children to the _____.
3 When he tried to drive the car onto the train, the guards _____.
4 Unfortunately, the train that he and his family were on was going _____.

GROUP C

a) Read Claire's postcard. Which picture does it describe?

b) Complete these sentences.

1 Claire wanted her holiday in the Caribbean to be _____.
2 There were problems with _____.
3 The tour they took was also bad because the taxi driver _____.
4 Unfortunately, she had to stay for two weeks although she _____.

3   Find a partner from each of the other groups and tell them 'your' story.

4   What bad holiday experiences have *you* had?

1 Maureen Lipman

Well, after the typhoons in Florida, the worst weather for 60 years in Tenerife, and two weeks of non-stop rain in Australia, I thought this was going to be different. I was the first person to get my bags at the airport – which usually never happens to me – and the hotel was excellent. Then the phone rang. 'Ms Lipman?' said a voice. 'Yes?' I said. 'I think I've got your suitcase,' said a voice.
Just going now to change the suitcase.
Love, Maureen

2 Leslie Thomas

Greetings from Italy! Confused? Here's why we're in Italy...
At the end of our French holiday I drove very fast to get the car, my wife and kids on the train to Boulogne. We were very late. I took them to the sleeper part and then I drove to a different place to put the car on the train. Well, the guard said I was too late. So I did the kind of thing I never do and drove through the men and onto the train. When an official came up to me, I said, 'I'm not moving.' 'Where are you going?' he asked. 'Boulogne,' I replied. 'Monsieur,' he said, 'this train is going to Milan.'
See you soon! Leslie

3 Claire Rayner

When we came to the Caribbean we were looking forward to a very comfortable holiday. But, it's awful. The hotel's terrible – the plughole in our washbasin isn't connected to the pipe and there's water all over the bedroom floor. I went for a swim in the pool and came face to face with a rat! We decided to take a tour. But the taxi driver wouldn't go faster than 5mph. Worst of all, we've booked for two weeks and can't get an early flight home, so we'll have to stay.
See you on the 10th, Claire

Mrs
14.
Lo
SE

Mr & N
159, B
Hove
East

Jane
25.
Sa
E

(from *Good Housekeeping*)

Listening

1   Read this extract from a questionnaire about holidays.
What do you like/dislike? Put the things in each list in the correct
order for you under A (1 = the things I like/dislike most).

LIKE	A You	B British people said	C %	DISLIKE	A You	B British people said	C %
1 Visiting museums and art galleries	—	—	—	1 Noisy and rude people	—	—	—
2 Spending more time with family and friends	—	—	—	2 Packing to go on holiday	—	—	—
3 Drinking a lot	—	—	—	3 Fighting to get a place by the pool	—	—	—
4 Seeing life in different countries	—	—	—	4 No information about delays	—	—	—
5 Enjoying the beauties of nature	—	—	—	5 Waiting at the airport	—	—	—
6 New kinds of food	—	—	—	6 Not speaking the language	—	—	—
7 Meeting new people	—	—	—	7 Traffic jams	—	—	—
8 Lying on the beach	—	—	—	8 Getting lost and arguing with each other	—	—	—
9 Just being away from home and the daily routine	—	—	—	9 Paying too much for things	—	—	—

2   What do British people like and dislike about holidays?

a) What do *you* think? Choose one thing from
each list.

b) [🖭 20.2]   Listen to the results of a survey
on holidays and the British. Were your
guesses correct?

c) Listen again. Put the things in each list in the
correct order for the British under B (1 = the
things they like/dislike most).

d) Listen again and complete the percentages (%)
under C.

Writing: linking words

Read about Posy Simmonds' experience and complete the
sentences. Use each word from the box once.

finally	and	but	so	when	then	because	after

Many years ago my husband,
his two sons and I stayed in
an awful hotel. The boys
and I got into the lift to go up to our
rooms _____ suddenly it stopped
_____ the lights went out.
_____ we smelt smoke _____ a
fire had started at the bottom below us.
We couldn't get out. Unfortunately,
_____ a kindly German took off
his shoe and broke the glass, more
smoke came in. _____ the power
came back on _____ the lift did not
go up. In fact, it shot down towards the
flames. Luckily the doors opened in
time _____ we got out safely.

Grammar

1 Mixed practice

Bill and Pat are at an exhibition of paintings and sculpture by the artist Pablo Picasso.

a) Which is the correct expression?

PAT: How long *are you / have you been* a fan of Picasso?

BILL: A long time. But I *haven't seen / didn't see* any of his paintings *for / since* the Paris exhibition in 1966. In those days I *used to find / find* it difficult to understand his work.

PAT: I *used to go / went* to an exhibition of his in New York, in 1973, the year he died. I *am / have been* waiting for an exhibition like this to come to London *for / since* years.

BILL: Me too.

PAT: Look at this sculpture of Jacqueline. It says in the programme that it *made / was made* by Picasso's assistants from a paper model.

BILL: Yes, it's *very / too* interesting. I like things *who / which* are a bit different.

PAT: I *said / told* Louise to come when she *has / will have* the time. I want *her to see / that she sees* some of these paintings.

BILL: Yes, Louise is *someone / anyone* who would like Picasso.

b) [📼 20.3] Listen and check your answers.

2 The Second Conditional

Join the sentences using a Second Conditional. Example:
I don't live in London. I don't go to the Tate Gallery.
If I lived in London, I would go to the Tate Gallery.

1 I don't know her address. I can't write to her.
2 She doesn't work. She hasn't any money.
3 I don't go swimming. I'm not fit.
4 I won't invite you to the theatre. I haven't got another ticket.
5 It is snowing. We can't go out.

3 Making comparisons

Complete the table.

ADJECTIVE	COMPARATIVE	SUPERLATIVE
good	better	_____
bad	_____	the worst
hardworking	_____	_____
happy	happier	_____
comfortable	_____	the most comfortable
big	_____	_____

4 Question tags

a) What is the question tag in each sentence?

1 There's something wrong, _____ ?
2 He likes jazz, _____ ?
3 She didn't try, _____ ?
4 It wasn't very nice, _____ ?
5 Tom's very attractive, _____ ?

b) [📼 20.4] Listen and check your answers.

Pronunciation

Weak forms and contractions

a) [📼 20.5] Listen to these sentences. How many words are there in each sentence? A contracted form (*he's*) is two words.

1 _____ you.
2 If _____ address _____.
3 I _____ rich.
4 He _____ watch _____ birthday.
5 How long _____ London?
6 Give _____ him _____.

b) Listen again and complete the sentences.

Vocabulary

1 Phrasal verbs

a) Replace the expressions in italics with a phrasal verb from the box. Put the phrasal verbs in the correct form. Example:
Phil *was Sue's boyfriend* for two years.
*Phil **went out with** Sue for two years.*

hang on	go out with	take off	break down
sell out	stay up	grow up	fill in
split up	look after		

1 Please *complete* this application form.
2 *Their relationship finished* last week. (They ...)
3 *Wait* a minute! Don't go.
4 I wanted to go to the football match but *there were no more tickets*. (The tickets were ...)
5 *Take care of* the children while I'm away.
6 If you are hot, *remove* your coat.
7 What do you want to do when you *are an adult* ?
8 My car *is not working*. (It has ...)
9 I *didn't go to bed* until midnight.

b) Complete the sentences with the correct form of one of the verbs in Exercise 1a).

1 When I arrived at the airport I had to *fill in an immigration form.*
2 We weren't tired so we decided to _____.
3 I was travelling to work when the train _____.
4 The class finishes in five minutes. Can you _____ ?
5 My brother's not very well. Can you _____ him?
6 You're like a child. Why don't you _____ ?

2 Correct or incorrect?

Are these sentences correct or incorrect? Tick or cross the first box. Then bet between 10 and 50 points on each: 50 points = you're sure you are right; 10 points = you're not sure you're right.
If you are right, you win the number of points you bet.
If you are wrong, you lose the number of points you bet.

	✓ / ✗	YOUR BET
1 Have you made your homework?	✗	40
2 He is very tall and handsome.	✓	50
3 She passed a degree at university.		
4 He won him at tennis.		
5 Have you joined the club?		
6 He was arrested for burglary.		
7 I enjoyed at the party.		
8 Did you play jogging yesterday?		
9 A pop star has been found shot dead.		
10 He's a very unhonest.		
11 She's a very good cycler.		
12 Have you been off work today?		

How many points have you won?

Use your English

What are these people saying? There is more than one answer.

Work with a partner and practise the conversations.

Writing

Sergio's teacher has underlined the mistakes in his homework. Rewrite the homework. Correct the underlined mistakes. Add any words and punctuation which are missing (⌀ means something is missing).

I usually <u>every summer go to the USA</u>. However, this year <u>i</u> went to <u>the</u> Greece <u>so</u> <u>i</u> wanted to see my friend <u>andreas</u>. Andreas looked very well. ⌀ <u>its</u> great to see you ⌀ he said. ⌀ Are you <u>comeing</u> to ⌀ Acropolis this evening? <u>its</u> beautiful at night. ⌀ <u>Although</u>, I told <u>he</u> I was a little tired. ⌀ <u>Lets</u> go tomorrow, ⌀ I said. <u>andreas</u> looked disappointed <u>because</u> I changed my mind. We went out and had a very happy evening.

LEARNING REVIEW

a) Which of these do you read or listen to in English outside the classroom?

Which is the most useful? Why? Which is the most difficult? Why?

b) Which of these are true for you outside the classroom?

- I look back at my vocabulary notes.
- I practise new words in sentences.
- I look at my grammar notes.
- I read the *Language reference* sections at the end of each Unit.

c) How much more practice do you need in these? Number them 1-7 (1 = I need the most practice).

- listening __
- speaking __
- reading __
- writing __
- grammar __
- vocabulary __
- pronunciation __

Additional material

Unit 11 (page 68)

Quiz answers
1 cheetah 3 giraffe   5 giraffe
2 rhino   4 elephant

Unit 12 (page 75)

GROUP A: 1 opera   2 Rome   3 Malay, Chinese, Tamil and English   4 at an American university in Cambridge, Mass.

GROUP B: 1 tennis   2 works of art (paintings and sculpture)   3 on a beach in Rio de Janeiro, Brazil   4 play it – it's a Russian musical instrument

Unit 12 (page 77)

Philip

John

Mary

Henry

Susan

STUDENT A
Look at the picture above. You are going to ask your partner five questions about the people.

First write your questions. Example:
Is Henry older than Susan?

a) Show your partner your picture. Ask him/her your questions.
b) Compare the people in the two pictures. Example:
I think Helen is the most attractive.

Unit 14 (page 87)

STUDENT A
You and your partner both have information about Keanu Reeves. Most of the information is the same, but you've got some information which your partner hasn't got. Use question tags to check and find the extra information. Example:
A: *He was born in 1965, wasn't he?*
B: *Yes, he was.*

KEANU REEVES

was born in Beirut in 1965. His mother is English. When he was young he wanted to be a racing driver. Keanu began acting when he was 18. He has played in the films *Dracula* and *Little Buddha*. Keanu loves riding motorbikes. He has got a 1974 Norton and drives at 130 mph.

Unit 16 (pages 99 and 128)

Quiz answers

GROUP A
1 McDonald's restaurants
2 the Portuguese
3 1945
4 J.L. Baird
5 rice
6 Norway

GROUP B
1 1953
2 31 October
3 The USA
4 Memphis
5 Shakespeare
6 France

Unit 14 (page 89)

STUDENT A

a) You and your partner have similar pictures. Ask questions and find ten differences. Don't look at your partner's picture and don't show him/her your picture.

b) Now look at your partner's picture and answer these questions.

1 What does the woman look like?
2 What kind of person do you think she is?
3 Where is she?
4 What is happening in the picture?

Unit 16 (page 100)

GROUP A

Look at the picture below. What do you think has happened? What is going to happen

Now work with a partner from Group B. Listen while your partner tells his/her part of the story. Don't look at your partner's picture. Then tell the story in your picture.

Unit 17 (page 107)

STUDENT A

a) What are the past participles of these verbs: write, see, be, buy, shut, teach, read, do, catch, eat?

b) Your partner is going to ask you about some past participles.

c) Ask your partner about the past participles of your verbs. Write down his/her answers. Don't say if the answer is correct or not. Example:
A: *What is the past participle of write?*
B: *Written.*

d) Check your answers on page 129. Who got the most correct answers?

Unit 18 (page 111)

STUDENT A
You are from the same family as Student B. Choose how you are related. Are you husband and wife, brother and sister or parent and child? You have had an argument. You are angry with Student B because he/she:

- gets up late
- doesn't help in the house
- borrows a lot of money

Make a list of other things you are angry about (money, parties, TV, clothes, car etc.) You aren't speaking to Student B but Student C is a go-between. Ask him/her to help you.

Unit 16 (page 99)

GROUP A
Look at the quiz below. Write full questions
for 4-6.

1 What was introduced into Russia on 2 March 1988?
   Mobile phones, McDonald's restaurants or credit cards?
2 Who was Brazil controlled by between 1500 and 1825?
   The Portuguese, the Spanish or the French?
3 When was the United Nations started? 1918, 1938 or
   1945?
4 Who/television invented by? G. Marconi, J.L. Baird or
   A. Bell?
5 What/Japanese drink sake/made from? Potatoes, rice
   or apples?
6 Where/Winter Olympics/held in 1994? Norway,
   Canada or Sweden?

Answer all the questions.
Check the answers on page 126.

2 Ask the other group your questions. The
group with the most correct answers wins.

Unit 20 (page 120)

STUDENT A
You are going to book into the Swan Hotel
for two weeks. It's very important that this
holiday goes well and everything is right for
you. What information do you want about the
hotel? Student A is the hotel's receptionist.
Ask him/her questions about: park/car? how
far/city centre?/TV? rooms with private
bathrooms? central heating? restaurant?
bring/dog? price?

Pronunciation: phonemic chart

CONSONANTS				VOWELS		DIPHTHONGS	
symbol	key word	symbol	key word	symbol	key word	symbol	key word
/ p /	**p**en	/ s /	**s**oon	/ iː /	s**ee**	/ eɪ /	m**a**ke
/ b /	**b**ack	/ z /	**z**oo	/ ɪ /	h**i**m	/ əʊ /	n**o**
/ t /	**t**ea	/ ʃ /	fi**sh**	/ e /	b**e**d	/ aɪ /	wr**i**te
/ d /	**d**ay	/ ʒ /	televi**si**on	/ æ /	b**a**d	/ aʊ /	n**ow**
/ k /	**k**ey	/ h /	**h**ot	/ ɑː /	c**ar**	/ ɔɪ /	b**oy**
/ g /	**g**et	/ m /	**c**ome	/ ɒ /	h**o**t	/ ɪə /	h**ere**
/ tʃ /	**ch**air	/ n /	su**n**	/ ɔː /	s**aw**	/ eə /	th**ere**
/ dʒ /	**j**ump	/ ŋ /	E**ng**lish	/ ʊ /	p**u**t	/ ʊə /	t**our**
/ f /	**f**at	/ l /	**l**amp	/ uː /	y**ou**		
/ v /	**v**ery	/ r /	**r**ed	/ ʌ /	c**u**t		
/ θ /	**th**ing	/ j /	**y**et	/ ɜː /	b**ir**d		
/ ð /	**th**en	/ w /	**w**et	/ ə /	Chin**a**		

Irregular verbs

VERB	PAST SIMPLE	PAST PARTICIPLE	VERB	PAST SIMPLE	PAST PARTICIPLE
be	was/were	been	leave	left	left
become	became	become	lend	lent	lent
begin	began	begun	lose	lost	lost
blow	blew	blown	make	made	made
break	broke	broken	mean	meant	meant
bring	brought	brought	meet	met	met
build	built	built	pay	paid	paid
burn	burned, burnt	burned, burnt	put	put	put
buy	bought	bought	read	read	read
catch	caught	caught	ride	rode	ridden
choose	chose	chosen	ring	rang	rung
come	came	come	run	ran	run
cost	cost	cost	say	said	said
cut	cut	cut	see	saw	seen
do	did	done	sell	sold	sold
draw	drew	drawn	send	sent	sent
dream	dreamed, dreamt	dreamed, dreamt	shake	shook	shaken
drink	drank	drunk	show	showed	shown, showed
drive	drove	driven	shut	shut	shut
eat	ate	eaten	sing	sang	sung
fall	fell	fallen	sit	sat	sat
feed	fed	fed	sleep	slept	slept
feel	felt	felt	speak	spoke	spoken
find	found	found	spell	spelt	spelt
fly	flew	flown	spend	spent	spent
forget	forgot	forgotten	stand	stood	stood
freeze	froze	frozen	steal	stole	stolen
get	got	got	swim	swam	swum
give	gave	given	take	took	taken
go	went	gone, been	teach	taught	taught
grow	grew	grown	tell	told	told
have	had	had	think	thought	thought
hear	heard	heard	throw	threw	thrown
hide	hid	hidden	understand	understood	understood
hit	hit	hit	wake	woke	woken
held	held	held	wear	wore	worn
keep	kept	kept	win	won	won
know	knew	known	write	wrote	written
learn	learned, learnt	learned, learnt			

Word list

This is a list of the most useful new words in each unit. *n* = noun *v* = verb *adj* = adjective *adv* = adverb

UNIT 11

acting (n) /'æktɪŋ/
bird-watching (n) /'bɜːd ˌwɒtʃɪŋ/
booking form (n) /'bʊkɪŋ fɔːm/
breathe (v) /briːð/
camping (n) /kæmpɪŋ/
car hire (n) /kɑː haɪə/
climb (v) /klaɪm/
complete (v) /kəm'pliːt/
date of birth (n) /ˌdeɪt əv 'bɜːθ/
departure (n) /dɪ'pɑːtʃə/
dive (n) /daɪv/
driving licence (n) /'draɪvɪŋ ˌlaɪsəns/
elephant (n) /'elɪfənt/
emotional (adj) /ɪ'məʊʃənəl/
fattening (adj) /'fætnɪŋ/
fill in (v) (to **fill in** a form) /fɪl 'ɪn/
giraffe (n) /dʒə'rɑːf/
good-looking (adj) /ˌgʊd 'lʊkɪŋ/
hang-gliding (n) /'hæŋ ˌglaɪdɪŋ/
hard-working (adj) /ˌhɑːd 'wɜːkɪŋ/
hobby (n) /'hɒbi/
ice skating (n) /'aɪs skeɪtɪŋ/
immigration (n) /ˌɪmɪ'greɪʃən/
join (v) (to **join** a club) /dʒɔɪn/
knitting (n) /'nɪtɪŋ/
length (n) /leŋθ/
nationality (n) /ˌnæʃə'nælɪti/
neck (n) /nek/
parachuting (n) /'pærəʃuːtɪŋ/
passport (n) /'pɑːspɔːt/
permanent (adj) /'pɜːmənənt/
purpose (n) /'pɜːpəs/
sales manager (n) /'seɪlz ˌmænɪdʒə/
short-sighted (adj) /ˌʃɔːt 'saɪtɪd/
signature (n) /'sɪgnɪtʃə/
snake (n) /sneɪk/
sociable (adj) /'səʊʃəbəl/
stamp-collecting (n) /'stæmp kəˌlektɪŋ/
stay (n) /steɪ/
surname (n) /'sɜːneɪm/
tiger (n) /'taɪgə/
ugly (adj) /'ʌgli/
waste (v) (to **waste** time) /weɪst/
water-skiing (n) /'wɔːtə ˌskiːɪŋ/

UNIT 12

accept (v) /ək'sept/
argument (n) /'ɑːgjʊmənt/
arrest (v) /ə'rest/
burglar (n) /'bɜːglə/
chilly (adj) /'tʃɪli/
commit (v) (to **commit** a crime) /kə'mɪt/
competition (n) /ˌkɒmpə'tɪʃən/
confess (v) /kən'fes/
crime (n) /kraɪm/
dial (v) /daɪəl/
evidence (n) /'evɪdəns/
explanation (n) /ˌeksplə'neɪʃən/
fall in love (v) /ˌfɔːl ɪn 'lʌv/
freezing (adj) /'friːzɪŋ/
horrified (adj) /'hɒrɪfaɪd/

improvement (n) /ɪm'pruːvmənt/
judge (n) /dʒʌdʒ/
microphone (n) /'maɪkrəfəʊn/
neighbour (n) /'neɪbə/
opinion (n) /ə'pɪnjən/
postcard (n) /'pəʊstkɑːd/
prison (n) /'prɪzən/
record (v) /rɪ'kɔːd/
robber (n) /'rɒbə/
saving (n) /'seɪvɪŋ/
steal (v) /stiːl/
thief (n) /θiːf/
towel (n) /'taʊəl/
upset (adj) /ʌp'set/
voice (n) /vɔɪs/
warning (n) /'wɔːnɪŋ/
witness (n) /'wɪtnɪs/

UNIT 13

adore (v) /ə'dɔː/
bad-tempered (adj) /bæd 'tempəd/
be fond of (v) /bi 'fɒnd əv/
blanket (n) /'blæŋkɪt/
buggy (n) /'bʌgi/
clever (adj) /'klevə/
corkscrew (n) /'kɔːkskruː/
crossroads (n) /'krɒsrəʊdz/
depend (v) /dɪ'pend/
dream (v) /driːm/
garlic (n) /'gɑːlɪk/
get married (v) /get 'mærid/
get pregnant (v) /get 'pregnənt/
glue (n) /gluː/
go out together (v) /gəʊ ˌaʊt tə'geðə/
interview (v) /'ɪntəvjuː/
lazy (adj) /'leɪzi/
leather (adj) /'leðə/
marriage (n) /'mærɪdʒ/
old-fashioned (adj) /ˌəʊld 'fæʃənd/
one-way street (n) /ˌwʌn 'weɪ ˌstriːt/
patient (adj) /'peɪʃənt/
pedestrian crossing (n) /pəˌdestriən 'krɒsɪŋ/
perfect (adj) /'pɜːfɪkt/
purse (n) /pɜːs/
roundabout (n) /'raʊndəbaʊt/
scarf (n) /skɑːf/
scissors (n) /'sɪzəz/
shoplift (v) /'ʃɒpˌlɪft/
shy (adj) /ʃaɪ/
straight (adj) (**straight** on) /streɪt/
T-junction (n) /'tiː ˌdʒʌŋkʃən/
talkative (adj) /'tɔːkətɪv/
traffic lights (n) /'træfɪk laɪts/
unnatural (adj) /ʌn'nætʃərəl/
vacuum cleaner (n) /'vækjʊəm ˌkliːnə/
wallet (n) /'wɒlɪt/
woollen (adj) /ˌwʊlən/

UNIT 14

amusing (adj) /ə'mjuːzɪŋ/
annual (adj) /'ænjuəl/
artist (n) /'ɑːtɪst/
audience (n) /'ɔːdiəns/
author (n) /'ɔːθə/
battery (n) /'bætəri/
behave (v) /bɪ'heɪv/
CD (n) /siː'diː/
circus (n) /'sɜːkəs/
clap (v) /klæp/
clerk (n) /klɑːk/
comedian (n) /kə'miːdiən/
composer (n) /kəm'pəʊzə/
concert (n) /'kɒnsət/
conductor (n) /kən'dʌktə/
confident (adj) /'kɒnfɪdənt/
deep (adj) /diːp/
drama (n) /'drɑːmə/
drawing (n) /'drɔːɪŋ/
energy (n) /'enədʒi/
exhibition (n) /ˌeksɪ'bɪʃən/
fan (n) (a pop **fan**) /fæn/
film director (n) /'fɪlm dəˌrektə/
front row (n) /ˌfrʌnt 'rəʊ/
headphones (n) /'hedfəʊnz/
interval (n) /'ɪntəvəl/
kidnap (v) /'kɪdnæp/
loudspeaker (n) /ˌlaʊd'spiːkə/
motorbike (n) /'məʊtəbaɪk/
musician (n) /mjuː'zɪʃən/
name (v) (to **name** a baby) /neɪm/
newsagent's (n) /'njuːzˌeɪdʒənts/
nicely (adj) /'naɪsli/
nurse (n) /nɜːs/
obsession (n) /əb'seʃən/
own (v) (to **own** a shop) /əʊn/
performance (n) /pə'fɔːməns/
pop group (n) /'pɒpgruːp/
racing driver (n) /'reɪsɪŋ ˌdraɪvə/
screen (n) /skriːn/
sculpture (n) /'skʌlptʃə/
shocking (adj) /'ʃɒkɪŋ/
show (n) (to see a **show**) /ʃəʊ/
stage (n) /steɪdʒ/
stereo system (n) /'steriəʊ ˌsɪstəm/
video recorder (n) /'vɪdiəʊ rɪˌkɔːdə/
video tape (n) /'vɪdiəʊ teɪp/
zoo (n) /zuː/

UNIT 15

attend (v) /əˈtend/
crazy (adj) (It's **crazy**) /ˈkreɪzi/
drugs (n) /drʌgz/
economics (n) /ˌekəˈnɒmɪks/
educate (v) /ˈedjʊkeɪt/
employer (n) /ɪmˈplɔɪə/
history (n) /ˈhɪstri/
inexpensive (adj) /ˌɪnɪkˈspensɪv/
IT (information technology) (n) /ˌaɪ ˈtiː
    (ˌɪnfəˈmeɪʃən tekˈnɒlədʒi) /
punish (v) /ˈpʌnɪʃ/
rule (n) /ruːl/
science (n) /ˈsaɪəns/
too (adv) /tuː/
top (n) /tɒp/
typing (n) /ˈtaɪpɪŋ/
uniform (n) /ˈjuːnɪfɔːm/

UNIT 16

alive (adj) /əˈlaɪv/
assassinate (v) /əˈsæsɪneɪt/
attack (v) /əˈtæk/
best-selling (adj) /ˌbest ˈselɪŋ/
blow up(v) (= explode) /bləʊ ˈʌp/
bomb (n) /bɒm/
celebrate (v) /ˈselɪbreɪt/
cloud (n) /klaʊd/
collapse (v) /kəˈlæps/
confused (adj) /kənˈfjuːzd/
cool (adj) /kuːl/
destroy (v) /dɪˈstrɔɪ/
dishonest (adj) /dɪsˈɒnɪst/
drunk (adj) /drʌŋk/
earthquake (n) /ˈɜːθkweɪk/
explosion (n) /ɪkˈspləʊʒən/
horoscope (n) /ˈhɒrəskəʊp/
incorrect (adj) /ˌɪnkəˈrekt/
invent (v) /ɪnˈvent/
light bulb (n) /ˌlaɪt bʌlb/
nonsense (n) /ˈnɒnsəns/
nonstop (adj) /ˌnɒn ˈstɒp/
nonstop (adv) /ˌnɒn ˈstɒp/
organise (v) /ˈɔːgənaɪz/
question (v) (to **question** somebody)
    /ˈkwestʃən/
razor blade (n) /ˈreɪzə bleɪd/
real (adj) /rɪəl/
smile (v) /smaɪl/
superb (adj) /suːˈpɜːb/
total (n) /ˈtəʊtl/
unkind (adj) /ʌnˈkaɪnd/
unluckily (adv) /ʌnˈlʌkɪli/
unpleasant (adj) /ʌnˈplezənt/
wave (v) /weɪv/
weather forecast (n) /ˈweðə ˈfɔːkɑːst/
youth (n) /juːθ/

UNIT 17

ban (v) /bæn/
calendar (n) /ˈkælɪndə/
Christian (adj) /ˈkrɪstʃən/
congratulations (n) /kənˌgrætʃəˈleɪʃənz/
cook (n) /kʊk/
cow (n) /kaʊ/
driving test (n) /ˈdraɪvɪŋ test/
faithful (adj) /ˈfeɪθfəl/
festival (n) /ˈfestɪvəl/
guest (n) /gest/
injured (adj) /ˈɪndʒəd/
lamp (n) /læmp/
last (v) /lɑːst/
lend (v) /lend/
live (adj) (**live** music) /laɪv/
monkey (n) /ˈmʌŋki/
non-alcoholic (adj) /ˌnɒn ˌælkəˈhɒlɪk
originally (adv) /əˈrɪdʒənəlɪ/
rabbit (n) /ˈræbɪt/
recorded (adj) /rɪˈkɔːdɪd/
religious (adj) /rɪˈlɪdʒəs/
revolution (n) /ˌrevəˈluːʃən/
sober (adj) /ˈsəʊbə/
soft drink (n) /sɒft ˈdrɪŋk/

UNIT 18

back door (n) /ˌbæk ˈdɔː/
be off (v) (to **be off** work) /bi ˈɒf/
come round (v) (= visit) /kʌm ˈraʊnd/
decorate (v) /ˈdekəreɪt/
dislike (v) /dɪsˈlaɪk/
drums (n) /drʌmz/
dust (v) /dʌst/
hoover (v) /ˈhuːvə/
iron (v) /ˈaɪən/
rubbish (n) /ˈrʌbɪʃ/
shopping (n) /ˈʃɒpɪŋ/
sip (v) /sɪp/
teabag (n) /ˈtiːbæg/
tidy up (v) /ˌtaɪdi ˈʌp/

UNIT 19

baseball (n) /ˈbeɪsbɔːl/
basketball (n) /ˈbɑːskɪtbɔːl/
beat (v) (Liverpool **beat** Chelsea) /biːt/
boo (v) /buː/
bounce (v) /baʊns/
cheat (n) /tʃiːt/
cheat (v) /tʃiːt/
crowd (n) /kraʊd/
disappear (n) /ˌdɪsəˈpɪə/
drop (v) /drɒp/
jogging (n) /ˈdʒɒgɪŋ/
kick (v) /kɪk/
be mad about (v) (= be very keen on)
    /bɪˈmæd əˈbaʊt/
message (n) /ˈmesɪdʒ/
nun (n) /nʌn/
passion (n) /ˈpæʃən/
poor (n) (the **poor**) /pʊə/
prayer (n) /preə/
punch (v) /pʌntʃ/
recently (adv) /ˈriːsəntli/
reporter (n) /rɪˈpɔːtə/
score (v) (to **score** a goal) /skɔː/
share (v) /ʃeə/
squash (n) (to play **squash**) /skwɒʃ/
swimming costume (n) /ˈswɪmɪŋ
    ˌkɒstjʊm/
swimming pool (n) /ˈswɪmɪŋ puːl/
team (n) /tiːm/
tennis court (n) /ˈtenɪs kɔːt/
tennis racket (n) /ˈtenɪs ˌrækɪt/
win (v) /wɪn/
windsurfing (n) /ˈwɪnd ˌsɜːfɪŋ/

UNIT 20

atmosphere (n) /ˈætməsfɪə/
central heating (n) /ˌsentrəl ˈhiːtɪŋ/
cocktail bar (n) /ˈkɒkteɪl bɑː/
daily routine (n) /ˌdeɪli ruːˈtiːn/
en-suite toilet (n) /ˌɒn ˈswiːt ˈtɔɪlət/
flame (n) /fleɪm/
nearby (adv) /ˌnɪəˈbaɪ/
power (n) (= electricity) /ˈpaʊə/
receptionist (n) /rɪˈsepʃənɪst/
residential area (n) /ˌrezɪˈdenʃəl ˈeərɪə/
smell (v) /smel/
traffic jam (n) /ˈtræfɪk dʒæm/
unpack (v) /ʌnˈpæk/

Tapescripts

Unit 11

RECORDING 2

PHILIP: Sarah and I don't spend our free time doing crosswords. We lead a very active life. When we're not working we enjoy rock-climbing or parachuting or going on safari in Africa. I've even learnt how to fly a plane. I suppose our favourite pastime though is deep-sea diving. Especially in the Caribbean. I remember once we took the boat into the Gulf of Mexico. The water wasn't very clear. We all went in except Jules. He stayed on the boat. There were some fantastic sights. Amazing creatures I'd never seen before. It was magic with the light on. A kind of wonderland. It wasn't very deep and we were near the bottom. Then all of a sudden I saw Sarah waving her arms at me. She looked frantic. I didn't realise what it was at first. I thought she couldn't breathe or something. Then I saw it. This incredible great shark coming towards me. I've never moved so fast in my life. Luckily, it wasn't interested in me. It just went straight past. Perhaps it wasn't a man-eater or it was short-sighted or something.

Unit 12

RECORDING 1

1 A: Nice to see you again.
   B: Hi! How are you? I hear you've not been very well.
   A: I'm fine now, thanks. How about you?

2 A: Hello, Sally.
   B: Hello. Thanks very much for Tom's present. It was just what he wanted.
   A: You're welcome.

3 A: Is Colin here?
   B: Colin who?
   A: You know. Colin Wilson. I want to see him.
   A: I don't think so. I haven't seen him.

4 A: It's a bit chilly today, isn't it?
   B: Yes, I think it's going to snow.
   A: I hope not. We're playing football later.

RECORDING 2

1 ANNOUNCER: Last night in Windsor a burglar broke into a house and stole a mobile phone. Later he rang the owner offering to sell it half-price for two hundred pounds...
2 Yesterday morning at Burnham a robber tied up a bank manager and took thousands of pounds. The bank manager dialled nine, nine, nine with his tongue and called the police. The police later arrested the robber.
3 A thief walked into an electrical shop in Hitchin and loaded a washing machine into his car. He calmly drove away. The man has been sent to prison for six months.

Unit 13

RECORDING 1

PENNY: Now listen carefully. When you come out of the station on to Waverley Bridge, turn right and go straight on until you get to Princes Street. Turn left and walk along Princes Street for about fifteen minutes. Go past the Royal Scottish Academy. You'll see the Castle and the Mound on your left. When you get to the end of Princes Street (you'll see the Caledonian Hotel in front of you), turn left again into Lothian Road. Walk straight along Lothian Road and after five minutes you'll see the Usher Hall on your left, opposite the Sheraton Hotel.

RECORDING 2

I feel it in my fingers
I feel it in my toes
Well, love is all around me
and so the feeling grows.
It's written on the wind,
It's everywhere I go.
So if you really love me
Come on and let it show.

RECORDING 3 (As Recording 2)
You know I love you,
I always will.
My mind's made up
By the way that I feel.
There's no beginning, there'll be no end
'Cos on my love, you can depend.

I see your face before me,
As I lay on my bed.
I kind of get to thinking,
Of all the things you said.
You gave your promise to me,
And I gave mine to you.
I need someone beside me,
In everything I do.

It's written on the wind
It's everywhere I go.
So if you really love me
Come on and let it show.

RECORDING 4

1 A: I met him last night. He works here. He's nearly bald and rather short.
   B: We have a lot of people here like that, sir.
   A: Well, he's got a round face with a pointed nose.
   B: I see.
   A: And a beard.
   B: Well, that could be Mr Page...

2 A: Yes, she's in her mid-twenties and really slim.
   POLICEWOMAN: Fine. Can you give me more details? What colour are her eyes?
   A: Let me see. Yes, she's got large green eyes.
   P: Yes, yes I'm sure. You say she's missing.
   A: Yes, she didn't come home...

3 A: Excuse me, I'm looking for my girlfriend.
  B: Oh, dear! Have you lost her?
  A: Yes, she's... eh... average height, not pretty... quite plain in fact... and a... eh... bit overweight I suppose.
  B: That's not a very nice way to talk about your girlfriend!
  A: Sorry... I mean... No... Let me think. She's got short curly hair with a square face, green eyes.
  B: I think I know who you mean. She was the person I saw getting on a plane for Paris with a very good-looking, wonderfully handsome man who looked like a film star...
  A: What?!

4 A: Excuse me. I'm looking for a friend of mine. I said I'd meet him here.
  B: What does he look like?
  A: Um... He's quite tall and well-built. And he's got long black hair. Oh yes, and he's got a beard and he wears glasses.
  B: Oh, him. Yes. He's in the lounge...

Unit 14

RECORDING 4

NIKKI: We're not going out tonight, are we?
TOM: No, let's not. I'm too tired. Let's see what's on TV.
N: Well, there's 'Star Trek' at 6.30. I'm a fan of William Shatner. He's a good actor, isn't he?
T: I don't like him very much. Let me have a look. 'Headhunters'. That sounds interesting.
N: I can't stand Francesca Annis.
T: Well, I want to watch it.
N: OK, we'll watch it if I can watch 'Star Trek'.
T: 'Panorama' doesn't sound very interesting this week.
N: And it wasn't very good last week, was it?
T: No. Let's see what else there is. You still like Sting, don't you? He's on.
N: Yes. I certainly want to watch him.
T: I think this wildlife programme's been on before. The one about the elephants. We've seen it, haven't we?
N: Yes, we have. I don't want to see that again.
T: What about Rory Bremner? You liked him last time, didn't you?
N: All right.
T: Yes, let's watch that, shall we?

Unit 15

RECORDING 2

KAREN: Well, the day starts at eight o'clock. You stop for lunch at twelve and then you leave school in the middle of the afternoon. Then you go home or do some sport.
RIE: School starts at half-past eight and we have to be there at about eight o'clock. It finishes at four o'clock in the afternoon but we have many different activities so we have to stay at school until seven o'clock every evening.

RECORDING 3

Group A

KAREN: We don't have very many rules at our school back in the States. The main rules are: no drugs, no smoking and no fighting, but there are crazy rules too like no wearing hats.
INTERVIEWER: What happens if someone breaks the rules?
K: Then you have to stay in the classroom at lunchtime which is crazy because you just spend your time talking to your friends. If you do something serious, like drugs, they call the cops.
I: Do you have to wear a uniform?
K: No, you can wear what you want but everybody wants to wear the latest fashions, which is crazy in school.
I: And are the teachers very strict?
K: No, not really. You can do what you want in class, talk in class, even when the teachers are talking. They don't really mind.
I: How does your school in America compare with your school in Britain?
K: In the States, you can do what you want when you want. You can miss classes – they don't really care – but here in England it's very strict and you have a lot more rules, a uniform and things like that.

RECORDING 4

Group B

INTERVIEWER: Are there many rules in your school in Japan?
RIE: Yes, a lot. For example, we have to wear a school uniform but we mustn't go to town in a uniform. We have to go home first and change into our normal clothes.
I: What's the uniform like?
R: The traditional Japanese school uniform is navy blue with a long skirt. Sometimes it's quite pretty, but no one likes it. The modern uniform with a short skirt is quite popular.
I: Do you have to work hard in your school?
R: Yes, very. And our teachers are very strict. If we don't study hard they punish us.
I: What kind of punishments do they give you?
R: We have to stay late after school and study. Sometimes the teachers phone our parents and our parents have to come to school.
I: Rie, how does your school in Japan compare with your school in Britain?
R: My school in Japan is a girls' school but here it is a mixed school. In Japan we have fifty students in one class and we stay in the same room all day. Here there are only twenty students and we have to move each lesson.

Unit 16

RECORDING 2

ANDREW: You didn't ring me last night.

NICOLA: Sorry?

A: I said you didn't ring me last night.

N: I know. I went back to work.

A: What was the problem?

PASSENGER: Sorry.

N: Oh, sorry. Are you trying to get off?

P: Yes.

N: I had to phone America.

A: Oh yes?

N: Yes. I had to talk to our American director. Why don't we meet tonight?

A: No, I don't think so.

N: Oh, damn! Why won't this work?

OFFICIAL: Can I have a look at your ticket? Sorry but this is out of date. Would you come with me?

N: Oh, no. Did I forget to buy a ticket?

Unit 17

RECORDING 1

1   A: Put this present under the tree.

   B: Oh, thanks!

   A: You mustn't open it until the morning.

   B: OK.

   A: And don't eat too much tomorrow.

   B: Impossible! I always do.

2   A: I want to see the fireworks.

   B: Oh, I'll come with you.

   C: Have a good time, you two! And be careful! Don't get too near the bonfire.

3   A: Have you made your resolutions yet?

   B: Yes, I'm going to give up smoking.

   A: What, again?!

4   A: Oh, what a horrible sight! Here take these sweets.

   B: Thanks very much. Thank you.

   A: Not at all. Now go away!

5   A: Darling.

   B: Yes?

   A: Who was that card from?

   B: I don't know. There's no name on it.

   H: You went very red when the postman came.

   W: Did I?

   H: Yes. It's not from your new boss, is it?

Unit 18

RECORDING 1

1   A: Are you all right?

   B: Oh, could you give me a hand with these, please?

   A: Sure. Where do you want them?

   B: I'm trying to get them to my car.

   A: OK.

2   A: I'm going into town. Shall I post those for you?

   B: No thanks, I'm not quite ready yet. Oh, but can you get me some stamps, please?

   A: Sure.

3   A: Damn! I need two fifty ps. I'm sorry to trouble you but have you got any change?

   B: I don't know. Let me have a look. Sorry. No. I've only got a five pound note.

4   A: Tom. Excuse me. Could you give me a push?

   B: Sorry?

   A: I said do you think you could give me a push?

   B: OK.

5   HUSBAND: Hello. Oh, little Oscar.

   NEIGHBOUR: Hello.

   WIFE: I hear you're going away.

   N: Yes, I am. Would you mind looking after Oscar for a few days?

   W: Ah! I'm afraid we're going away too. Sorry.

RECORDING 2

Group A

HENRY: The music's so loud – thump, thump, thump, nearly every night. It gives me headaches and I have to lie down. I've been off work because of the noise. You can't imagine having a headache and hearing that noise. Sometimes I get really angry. The other night I went into the garden and shouted 'Shut up'. I phoned the police but they said they couldn't do anything. A lot of young people come and go. Sometimes they come into my garden and move my pot plants. Or knock on my front door. I don't mind if they have a good time but there has to be a limit. If they're going to have a party, at least they could tell me and I'd go out. It used to be very quiet round here.

RECORDING 3

Group B

TIM: It's sad that we are annoying this man next door. We had no idea. Sure we like music in the day and we sometimes have loud parties. But we've never had any trouble. If anyone wants to complain they can always come round. We're not going to get into a fight. I play loud music to wake myself up. About ten in the morning that's when it's the loudest. Yes, another person here plays very loud music but not all the time. Me I play music quietly when I'm up. I haven't had a party for six months. I'm surprised Mr Skitt is bothered. Perhaps he doesn't like the kind of music. Heavy metal or rap. I hear Mr Skitt's TV all the time and I hear him shouting at his cats but that's what you get if you live close to people. We obviously have a different way of life. I play the drums but I try not to be too loud. That's why I play them in the cellar.

Unit 19

RECORDING 1

1 ZOE: In a formal situation you should shake hands and say 'Nice to meet you' or 'How do you do.' We don't usually kiss people when we first meet them.

2 Always order at the bar. Take your drinks and sit down where you can find a seat. Here people sometimes share a table. To get food you usually order at the bar, too. There aren't usually any waiters although sometimes they will bring you your food.

3 Don't forget to ask before you have a bath or a shower. And try not to spend too long in the bathroom!

4 Never clap your hands or hit your glass with a knife. Say 'Excuse me!' or try to catch the waiter's eye.

5 People normally expect you to be a few minutes late. Never arrive early. Usually you have drinks before the meal. After you eat, you usually sit around chatting for a while. If you want to leave soon after the meal make sure you say you've had a lovely evening and the food was delicious and then make an excuse.

RECORDING 2

FATHER: What are you going to do when you get there?

TIM: I'll go straight to the hotel. I'll probably be very tired.

M: How will we know that you're all right?

T: Oh, Mum. Don't worry. I'll call you as soon as I can.

F: Then make sure you phone your uncle. Have you got your traveller's cheques?

T: Yes, Dad.

M: What will you do if he's not there when you phone? He won't know you're at the hotel.

T: I'll try again later. It'll be OK.

F: He won't come and pick you up unless you phone.

T: I know. Please don't worry.

M: Have you got everything? Have you packed your woollen socks and your big jumper?

T: Yes.

M: And your uncle's present. Don't forget. Give it to him as soon as you see him.

T: Yes.

Unit 20

RECORDING 2

ANNOUNCER: According to the latest survey the British still like their holidays. These are the results. 90% enjoy the beauties of nature and the countryside and 89% like being away from home and the daily routine. The same number – 89% like spending more time with the family and friends. This was surprising. In fact, according to the survey, family holidays seem to be good for family relationships. These are the other figures about what the British like. 88% of the British people we asked, like meeting new people and 87% like seeing life in different countries. A lot of people think the British don't like meeting new people but according to this survey this is not true. New kinds of food interested 79% of the people and 60% were mainly interested in lying on the beach and getting a suntan. Most people admit to putting on weight on holiday. Going to museums and art galleries interested only 58% and even fewer – a surprising 35% – just like drinking a lot. On the other hand, what people most dislike about their holidays is the journey. In particular not having information about why they have been delayed – 76% – while 72% hate any kind of waiting at the airport. The same number – 72% – hate traffic jams. The journey is often the most difficult part of the holiday. These are the other figures about what the British dislike. 58% of people hate paying too much for something and 56% hate noisy or rude people. However, 46% of the people we asked, complain about getting lost and arguing with each other and 37% say they hate fighting to get a place by the swimming pool. At the bottom of the list only 32% worry about not speaking the language – we think this would be different for other nationalities – and 27% hate packing. The survey suggests that the British like being with other people more than we think. Interestingly, more than a quarter arrive home as tired as or more tired than when they went.

Acknowledgements

We are grateful to the following for permission to reproduce copyright material:

The authors, Tessa Boase & Tom Hodgkinson for an extract from their article 'I'm a Real Fan' in *The Daily Telegraph* 19.11.93; the Author's Agent for the *Daily Mail* article 'How to eat spaghetti' by Antonio Carluccio in *Daily Mail* 30.10.93 © 1993; the Author's Agent for adapted extracts from *George's Marvellous Medicine* by Roald Dahl (publ. Jonathan Cape Ltd & Penguin Books Ltd); Ewan Macnaughton Associates for the adapted article 'Light Snack' in *The Daily Telegraph* 17.07.93; EMAP Woman's Group Ltd for an adapted extract from the article 'Want to be together forever?' in *New Woman* February, 1994; The Guardian for adapted extracts from the articles 'A Corner of Japan forever Cotswold' by Michael Prestage in *The Guardian* © 19.04.94, and 'Urban myths: call me mother' by Healey & Glanvill in *The Guardian Weekend* © 30.10.93; The National Magazine Company Ltd for an adapted extract from the article 'Postcards from the Edge' in *Good Housekeeping* magazine, September 1992 © National Magazine Company; Newspaper Publishing plc for adapted extracts from the articles 'She delivers kindness with the pintas' by Susan de Muth in *The Independent* 8.12.93, 'Daily bread' by Deborah Bull in *The Independent on Sunday* 14.11.93, and 'Barbra and her funny girl fans' by David Lester in *The Independent on Sunday* 10.04.94; Polygram International Music Publishing Ltd for the lyrics 'Love is All Around' written by Reg Presley © 1967 Dick James Music Ltd; Solo Syndication Ltd for adapted extracts from the articles ' A Lion with roar energy' by Graham Bridgstock in *Evening Standard* 18.01.94, 'Should we ever ask a police-woman to play seductress just to win a case?' by Geoffrey Levy in *Daily Mail* 12.03.94, 'Age of consent' by Marina Cantacuzino in *Daily Mail* 18.02.93, 'Inside story Carol Thatcher' by Clare Campbell in *Daily Mail Weekend* 22.1.94 and 'Wing and a Prayer' by Simon Kinnersley in *Mail on Sunday* 06.03.94; The Observer for an adaptation of the questionnaire 'Are You a Workaholic', p58 in the *Observer Colour Supplement* © The Observer; the author, David Thomas for an adapted extract from his article 'Nick and Kate Moss' in *The Daily Telegraph* 15.10.93.

We have unfortunately been unable to trace the copyright holder of the article 'Healthstyle Extra: Paul Smith' in *The Sunday Express Magazine* October 1989 and would appreciate any information which would enable us to do so.

We are grateful to the following for permission to reproduce copyright photographs:

Ace Photo Agency/Crysse Morrison for page 102MR; Allsport (UK) Ltd for page 115T; Alton Towers for page 48B; Austine J. Brown/Aviation Picture Library for page 48T; The Bridgeman Art Library/©D.A.C.S for page 42(a); Camera Press Ltd/Denzil McNeelance for page 19L & R, /Richard Open for page 25(A); J Allan Cash Ltd for page 54(1), 109(main); Comstock Photolibrary for page 91L; Greg Evans Photolibrary for page 12(a & d), 50TR, 54(3); Tim Graham-London for page 15; The Ronald Grant Archive for page 79; Robert Harding Picture Library for page 30(b & c), 34(b), 68(h), 54(2), 60M, /Martyn F. Chillmaid for page 43TM, /Ian Griffiths for page 34(d), /Adam Woolfitt for page 12(c), 43TR; Hulton Deutsch for page 29TL & B, 60B, /David Eason for page 29TR; The Image Bank for page 102ML, /Alan Becker for page 12(b), /G. Coliva for page 13(inset), /Joe Devenney for page 102TL, /Romilly Lockyer for page 102TR, /G & M David De Lossy for page 91(inset); The Independant/Geraint Lewis for page 85(B), /Susan de Muth for page 49; Ink Group Publishers for page 16; Katz Pictures ©1992 for page 86; The Kobal Collection for page 6T & M, 117(inset); ©Longman Group/Gareth Boden for page 14, 24, 36, 40T & (a-c), 42TL, 75R, 88, 92, 93L, 96(a & b), 102BR, 109(inset), /Trevor Clifford for page 10(c & e), 18, 30(d & e), 40(d), 42(b & c), 45, 75L, 118, 125; ©Lufthansa for page 10(b); Mail Newspapers/Solo Syndication for page 56, 115M; Mirror Syndication for page 78; The Moviestore Collection for page 6B, 117T; M.O.M.I for page 48LM; PhotoBank for page 91R; Press Association/Rebecca Naden for page 102BL(inset); Retna Pictures/John Atashian for page 85T, /Onyx for page 87; Rex Features Ltd for page 7, 25(B), 37, /Brooker for page 60T; The Royal Ballet/Anthony Crickman for page 40B; ©Bill Sanderson for page 61; Tony Stone Images for page 68(f), /Andy Cox for page 43TL, /Tony Craddock for page 10(a), /Dale Durfee for page 17(1), /David H. Endersbee for page 102BL, /Ken Fisher for page 17(2), /John Garrett for page 10(d), /Janet Gill for page 120,/Chris Harver for page 68(c), /Stephen Krasemann, /Tom Parker for page 54(4), /Manoj Shah for page 68(d & g), /Hugh Sitton for page 34(e), /Art Wolfe for page 50TL; Telegraph Colour Library for page 13(main), 34(a), 93R, /Bavaria Bildagentur for page 34(c), /M. Krasowitz for page 91R(inset), /Dia Max for page 30(a), /Planet Earth/Steve Bloom for page 68(e), Planet Earth/Linda Pitkin for page 48UM, Planet Earth/Jonathan Scott for page 68(a), /Tom Wilson for page 26.

Illustrated by

1-11 Line Art (Maps), Kathy Baxendale (h/w), Julia Bigg (The Inkshed), Paul Davies (Garden Studio), Stephen Dell, Andrew Farmer (Edinburgh map), Ramsay Gibb (Beint & Beint), Michael A Hill, Rod Holt, Lorna Kent, Harry North, Panteus Palios, Eric Smith, Graham Thompson, Lis Watkins (Pennant), Gary Wing, Allen Wittert (Pennant).

Cover illustration by Zap Art.